CW00540392

Identity and idolatry

NEW STUDIES IN BIBLICAL THEOLOGY 36

Series editor: D. A. Carson

Identity and idolatry

THE IMAGE OF GOD AND ITS INVERSION

Richard Lints

APOLLOS

INTERVARSITY PRESS

DOWNERS GROVE, ILLINOIS 60515

APOLLOS
An imprint of Inter-Varsity Press, England
Norton Street
Nottingham NG7 3HR, England
ivpbooks.com
ivp@ivpbooks.com

InterVarsity Press, USA
P.O. Box 1400
Downers Grove, IL 60515-1426, USA
ivpress.com
email@ivpress.com

*InterVarsity Press®, USA, is the book-publishing division of InterVarsity Christian Fellowship/
USA® and a member movement of the International Fellowship of Evangelical Students. Website:
intervarsity.org.*

*Inter-Varsity Press, England, is closely linked with the Universities and Colleges Christian
Fellowship, a student movement connecting Christian Unions throughout Great Britain, and a
member movement of the International Fellowship of Evangelical Students. Website: uccf.org.uk.*

Scripture quotations, unless otherwise noted, are from The Holy Bible, English Standard Version,
copyright © *2001 by Crossway Bibles, a division of Good News Publishers. Used by permission. All
rights reserved.*

First published 2015

Set in Monotype Times New Roman
Typeset in Great Britain by CRB Associates, Potterhanworth, Lincolnshire
Printed in Great Britain by 4edge Limited

USA ISBN 978-0-8308-2636-0 (print)
USA ISBN 978-0-8308-9849-7 (digital)
UK ISBN 978-1-78359-306-4

 *As a member of the Green Press Initiative, InterVarsity Press is committed to
protecting the environment and to the responsible use of natural resources. To learn
more, visit greenpressinitiative.org.*

British Library Cataloguing in Publication Data
A catalogue record for this book is available from the British Library.

Library of Congress Cataloging-in-Publication Data
A catalog record for this book is available from the Library of Congress.

P 21 20 19 18 17 16 15 14 13 12 11 10 9 8 7 6 5 4 3 2 1
Y 33 32 31 30 29 28 27 26 25 24 23 22 21 20 19 18 17 16 15

To Ann:
The light of my life in whose reflection the gospel shines clear

Contents

Series preface

New Studies in Biblical Theology is a series of monographs that address key issues in the discipline of biblical theology. Contributions to the series focus on one or more of three areas: (1) the nature and status of biblical theology, including its relations with other disciplines (e.g. historical theology, exegesis, systematic theology, historical criticism, narrative theology); (2) the articulation and exposition of the structure of thought of a particular biblical writer or corpus; and (3) the delineation of a biblical theme across all or part of the biblical corpora.

Above all, these monographs are creative attempts to help thinking Christians understand their Bibles better. The series aims simultaneously to instruct and to edify, to interact with the current literature and to point the way ahead. In God's universe mind and heart should not be divorced: in this series we will try not to separate what God has joined together. While the notes interact with the best of scholarly literature, the text is uncluttered with untransliterated Greek and Hebrew, and tries to avoid too much technical jargon. The volumes are written within the framework of confessional evangelicalism, but there is always an attempt at thoughtful engagement with the sweep of the relevant literature.

Those who know him have long appreciated the ability of Richard Lints to think creatively while remaining soaked in joyful confessionalism. Begin with the *imago Dei*, which in times past has often been thought of in terms of essential characteristics or attributes, but which is here thought of in terms of a mirror reflecting God and of subtle differences that stand over against him, making relationship with him possible – in short, establishing our identity with respect to God. Work that out across the canon, and you discover that light shines on many topics, not least the nature of idolatry. This book manages to blend some elements of systematic theology with careful biblical theology to produce a study that is wonderfully evocative.

D. A. Carson
Trinity Evangelical Divinity School

Author's preface

'Identity' is a term with a thousand different connotations but few know its precise denotation. What after all is identity? What makes me, me? What makes you, you? This book grew out of the conviction that the more we try to answer that question straightforwardly, the less likely we are to answer it at all. The irony of identity is that by looking away from ourselves we are more likely to discover our identity. Part of that is the complexity of self-identity itself. Part of it is the difficulty of genuine self-awareness. And part of it is the mystery of being created as people who find their identity in their capacity to reflect the Creator and the created order. This book is centrally about that mystery.

No simple description captures all of who we are, nor of the many influences that have been woven into our character. So it is with this book. Its origins lie almost too far back in the past to recover and record them faithfully. A seminar here. A hallway conversation there. A dinner table discussion with my family. Reading Genesis with a new set of eyes. Realizing how important the golden calf story is, but for reasons quite different from what I had originally thought. Finding the most incisive analysis of idolatry in the writings of the most acerbic critic of religion in the nineteenth century. Researching the rise of the modern marketing industry and recognizing how clearly it illustrates the design of the created order. Watching contemporary films and the fascination with the management of impressions that is at the heart of the film world. All of these, and more, pulled me in a thousand different directions when it was time to think about personal identity, but strangely also focused my attention on the Scriptures more sharply than I could have imagined. This book is an attempt to pull together many threads by following one of them from the beginning and seeing it through to its conclusion. That thread is nothing other than the way in which the Bible speaks about our identity as an image and reflection. From that simple origin I hope this work takes you on a journey of surprising discoveries.

This book is also a reflection of many influences in my own life and work. The conceptual origins of the book go back to the work (and friendship) of Meredith G. Kline. He taught me to see the text as a whole – and never to miss the forest for the trees. I will never forget the significance of that persistent voice of Meredith. One of Meredith's students and now one of my colleagues, Cathy McDowell, has written a remarkable dissertation on the early chapters of Genesis that further opened my eyes to these words of Scripture that speak powerfully to the 'the forest and the trees' of personal identity. Many others also reinforced that redemptive-historical, biblical-theological, big picture way of reading Scripture. Henri Blocher, Gordon Hugenberger, T. David Gordon, Greg Beale, D. A. Carson and Royce Greunler come very quickly and fondly to mind. Dear friends Michael Horton, Kelly Kapic and Paul Lim insisted that the best biblical theology would also be that which interacted with the wider world of critical scholarship. I hope they see their finger-prints all over this book. Long-time colleague David Wells as well as conversation partners Dick Keyes and Os Guinness taught me the inextricable connection between personal identities and cultural identities – which is also the heart of Scripture's conception of identity. Many of my students across the years have contributed to this work in explicit and mostly implicit ways. Brannin Pitre, Blake Arnoult and Derek Baker come immediately to mind across the last decade, as does Daniel Paik this past year, who laboured to put the indexes together.

Closer to home there is little doubt that my own reflections on personal identity are bound up with my identity in the context of my family. Kate and Lucas and Sarah and now Nathan have been surprising mirrors for me, helping me to see myself more clearly than I could ever otherwise have hoped for. They have learned not only to laugh with me but at me, and have thereby helped me not to take myself too seriously. They are adept at raising their eyebrows when my attempt at parental persuasion overreaches the argument itself. I trust that I am more comfortable in my own skin because they have unconditionally accepted me – even if that unconditional acceptance sometimes comes with disagreements.

This book would not have seen the light of day had not my best friend, co-worker and wife kept the flame alive – and made sure I took time off from administrative responsibilities to finish it. Mostly this has meant squeezing a half day here and a couple of hours there, all of it in between the relentless crush of a Dean's schedule. But she has not only kept the book alive; she has made it a much better book than I could ever have hoped it would be. I hope she will see all of the many refractions of her image in its prism. And for persevering through thirty winters in New England (2015 being the worst) there are not words of gratitude that will do her justice. May this book be a small token of that gratitude. For that reason and a thousand more this book is dedicated to her.

Richard Lints
February 2015

Abbreviations

ACCS	Ancient Christian Commentary on Scripture
ANE	ancient Near East(ern)
AUSS	*Andrews University Seminary Studies*
BJRL	*Bulletin of the John Rylands University Library of Manchester*
CBQMS	Catholic Biblical Quarterly Monograph Series
ERT	*Evangelical Review of Theology*
EvQ	*Evangelical Quarterly*
ExAud	*Ex auditu*
FUQ	*Free University Quarterly*
HKAT	Handkommentar zum Alten Testament
HBT	*Horizons in Biblical Theology*
HUCA	*Hebrew Union College Annual*
IBC	Interpretation: A Bible Commentary for Teaching and Preaching
Int	*Interpretation*
JBL	*Journal of Biblical Literature*
JETS	*Journal of the Evangelical Theological Society*
JR	*Journal of Religion*
JSNT	*Journal for the Study of the New Testament*
JSS	*Journal of Semitic Studies*
JTS	*Journal of Theological Studies*
NAC	New American Commentary
NICNT	New International Commentary on the New Testament
NIDNTT	*New International Dictionary of New Testament Theology*, ed. C. Brown, vol. 2, Grand Rapids: Zondervan, 1976
NovT	*Novum Testamentum*
NS	new series
NTS	*New Testament Studies*
OTL	Old Testament Library
RevExp	*Review and Expositor*

SBLDS	Society of Biblical Literature Dissertation Series
SBLSP	*Society of Biblical Literature Seminar Papers*
StVTQ	*St. Vladimir's Theological Quarterly*
Them	*Themelios*
TrinJ	*Trinity Journal*
TynB	*Tyndale Bulletin*
WBC	Word Biblical Commentary
WTJ	*Westminster Theological Journal*

Chapter One

Living inside the text: canon and creation

Her name was Simone. She had the face of Audrey Hepburn and the smile of Lauren Bacall. Her body looked like it had been sculpted by an artist. She moved like Madonna. She was an actress with breathtaking presence but little dramatic ability. Her Greta Garbo-like allure seemed to more than make up for her lack of acting talent. No one seemed to notice her stiffness on the big screen. She simply overshadowed every other actor and actress who appeared with her in films. Her image was just too much to compete with. By all accounts she was too good to be true. And in fact she was – she was the computer generated figment of her director's imagination. In the 2002 film of the same name Simone was an actress without flaws (except a lack of talent) created for the silver screen by sophisticated computer code.[1] No one inside the film realized this until it was too late, until even reality couldn't dissuade them from believing in her. She became larger than life to the audience inside the film though the audience outside the film is overly aware of the satire playing out before their eyes. Poking fun at the ability of films to create an alternative reality while presenting that alternative reality for our simple enjoyment is part of the narrative intention of the film. The audience in the theatre quickly realizes what the audience inside the film does not – but in doing so the external audience is itself unaware of the 'film' in which their ordinary lives play out as well. Surrounded by images that have captured their imagination, they may confess to believe in truth but often they simply believe what they want to believe. Being conscious of the way in which others are captured by images is no guarantee of the discernment needed to realize one's own captivity. Playing on this ambiguity is the reason why modern film has had such a powerful role in the contemporary world.

Film-making in the post-Disney age has made us aware of the power of images, especially when they are not connected to reality.

---

[1] Niccol 2002.

These alternative universes invite us to suspend judgment for a time, eventually disorienting us to the point where the lines between myth and reality become difficult to distinguish. Classic mythology carried this same intention, as have novels in every era. We are drawn into these narratives supposing at the outset that we are leaving reality behind, only to be caught inside a story that reorients us to its plot line and values. We are introduced to an alternative set of perceptions about what matters and why. This happens not only in fictional works, but also in any work of literature or film that perceives the world differently from the way we do. The works may be gritty and realistic portrayals of life from the vantage point of those who stand in other shoes than our own, or they may represent images of life very close to our own but whose consequences are different from the way we suppose they should be. The common thread is that these are not merely presentations of alternative facts, but alternative perceptions about the way the world is. And these alternative perceptions become intelligible when they are wrapped within universes of meaning – when they connect dots across a wide set of perceptions. These sorts of perceptions or images are powerful in so far as the patterns emerging from the dots resonate with us. Asking why the patterns resonate is to ask about the way we humans are wired for meaning.

The power of images to shape and reshape our perceptions is not new to our age but neither is it without a unique ethos in our age.[2] The age of marketers is peculiarly modern, but the age of competing perceptions is as old as civilization. The technological capacities of contemporary film-makers is without precedent, but the crafting of imaginative universes is as ancient as the Homeric gods. Humans have always lived with competing accounts of reality, but there can be little doubt that the amount of competition among alternative visions has reached epic proportions in our time. And with the rise in the conflicts of perceptions has come a renewed attention to the manner in which our self-identity both shapes and is shaped by those perceptions.

It is naive to suppose that the world has changed but our human identities have remained relatively unchanged. The world may be filled with technological innovations undreamt of a hundred years ago, for example the Internet and advanced medical technologies, but greater change has occurred in how we relate to that world, what we think

---

[2] See Stevens 1998 for an extended cultural argument about the decline of the written word and the ascendancy of the image in the last two centuries.

about ourselves and the ways in which our religious convictions have been compartmentalized inside our self-identities.

Equally naive is the supposition that there is nothing enduring about human identity, that all of what it means to be human is fluid. Whether from a strict evolutionary naturalism, or from a cosmic pessimism about the modern world, there are those who cannot see important analogies of human existence across the diverse ages and communities of humans. They may suppose that we are on the mythological road of progress or by contrast on the certain road of corruption by the modern world. What they share is the conviction that human nature is primarily a reflection of the culture in which they are embedded. But there are fixed points that tie us together and about which our classic religious convictions seek to make sense. God has made us in his image and that imprint in some sense has persisted across the ages and across our differences. Cultural influences are important but an enduring human identity is not thereby dissolved under the conditions of modernity.[3] Or so the biblical witness amply testifies.

To speak of the social shape of reality is to speak of the diverse ways in which our perceptions of reality function to shape the realities we are perceiving. Our expectations influence what we see and what we hear. Our assumptions about life influence how we listen to politicians as well as friends. Simone was created by a director in his own image with the expectation that she would act and speak as every actress should – that is to say, how he would like every actress to behave. She speaks his words. She acts out his intentions. She is his virtual image except that she happens to be a different gender, much more pleasing to the eyes and never frustrating to those around her. Her iconic status takes on a life of its own in the film inside the film. She becomes so idolized by her fans, and thus by her Creator, that her (un)reality becomes the controlling force over them. Eventually, in a desperate act aimed at regaining control, the director 'kills' Simone, only to find that her adoring fans refuse to admit to this fact and have him imprisoned for his malicious and murderous intention. Their entertainment has become more important than justice itself, or perhaps their entertainment has become the new basis of justice. The film plot is so outrageous that we fixate on its fictional and satirical quality even while laughing in a knowing way about how close to home it hits.

[3] Lints 2000: 91–110.

19

We shape the identities of those around us by seeing them through our filters. We listen to them with our expectations. We tell their stories through our own narrative. Normally these actions are not so outrageous that we forget that others are not simply images of our own creation, but we are often lulled into thinking that our own act of 'shaping' is mostly innocent and trivial. And often we cannot tell when this has happened, though we can spot it clearly when others perpetrate these distortions.

The social dimension of our identities and perceptions points at the fact that our relationships (visual, virtual, personal, communal) profoundly influence our identities.[4] We are creatures inside a social dynamic. That dynamic consists of a set of perceptions about the way the world is, perceptions that belong to us individually and corporately. That is to say, we not only have perceptions but are influenced by them. From one angle we may say the self is an ongoing conversation between our perceptions. Self-consciousness is that sense we have that we are both subjects (who have perceptions) and objects (which are perceived). The great mystery is that we can experience ourselves simultaneously as objects and subjects.[5] It is as if there are two people running around inside us – one that views others and one that views how others view us.[6] We take clues from ourselves and give clues to ourselves.

The clues we receive may well be peculiarly modern and deeply secular today but the persistent realities of our identities precede the modern era and will last beyond this present age.[7] We reflect the world we live in and the God who made us. The mystery of this double reflection is very much a part of the complex narrative of the Scriptures. It is what makes us both fragile and fixed in our identities. There

---

[4] Karl Barth's (1975) discussion is often cited as the locus for this renaissance of relational or trinitarian discussions of personhood. Grenz (2001) offers a nice summary of this and its impact upon theological questions of personhood. From a popular cultural vantage point with roughly corresponding consequences see Brooks 2012.

[5] A contemporary philosopher of mind in the Islamic tradition (Fatoorchi 2008: 29) writes in a similar vein, 'Consciousness is at once the most obvious feature of our mental life and the most mysterious.'

[6] The old dictum 'Talk to yourself; don't just listen to yourself' captures this dynamic of self-identity.

[7] Berger (1967: 3) writes, 'Every individual biography is an episode within the history of society, which both precedes and survives it. Society was there before the individual was born and it will be there after they have died. What is more, it is within society, and as a result of social processes, that the individual becomes a person, that he attains and holds onto an identity, and that he carries out the various projects that constitute his life. Persons cannot exist apart from society. The two statements that society is the product of persons and that persons are the product of society, are not contradictory.'

is an explanation for the character of our identities as fragile and fixed in the Scriptures themselves if we pay attention. The conceptual categories of the canon offer substantive help in understanding ourselves, as one might expect if the author of the canon were the Creator of the universe, who not only created all that is but also established its meaning. As a divine being who writes and speaks, this same God constitutes his creation in such a fashion that his categories of understanding are 'built into' that creation. Put succinctly, we are the way we are because God is the way he is, and we are the way we are because we are not God.

When God creates, he creates contexts reflective of his character. The analogies of his character are naturally found in the created order. The authors of Scripture do not merely create apt analogies to/for God from their own world of experience as they write about him. Language of God is not in the first instance simply derived reflections of human experience. God puts the analogies into creation as the divinely appointed means of understanding him.[8] The God who speaks, creates beings who speak, though they do not speak identically to their Creator. With words, they create worlds of meaning, but the creature's words do not sovereignly call reality into being as does the divine word. Verbal and visual images communicate meaning into the created order as well. Marriage is a metaphor of divine fidelity throughout the Scriptures precisely because God ordained marriage as just such an analogy in the created order. Marriage is also an 'image' within which husbands and wives carry on a distinctive relationship. That image of marriage is influenced from a variety of quarters in any culture. In the modern world those images come from many diverse quarters, and the problem of conflicting images then serves as a difficult interpretative problem for couples. It can also disorientate us in thinking about divine fidelity and divine compassion, even as divine fidelity serves as a prophetic corrective to human experiences of infidelity.[9]

The God who creates constitutes his creation in such a fashion that the categories of our understanding of him are 'hardwired' into our being. Without filling out this account with many details just yet, the natural reflection of God in the created order and in human creatures in particular serves as the beginning of the biblical account of the *imago Dei*. Humans are created as images of God. There is nothing

---

[8] Ward 2002.
[9] T. Hart 2000: 334–337.

complex about this claim nor is it filled with much conceptual baggage at the beginning of the canon of Scripture. It is primarily a methodological point. As a book enacting a mega-narrative between God and his creatures, the reflections (and distortions thereof) between humankind and God are woven into the fabric of the story itself. These reflections allow the story to make the divine–human interactions intelligible.

A conceptual linkage between God and humans is one of reflection – so the opening chapters of Genesis claim. It is quite obviously more than that, but there is a surprising silence as to the substance of this reflection and thereby the restraints it places on our speculations about human identity. But that humans reflect God does not go far towards saying how they do and do not reflect him. There is little cash value in the claim itself. There is virtually no content placed in the conceptual construct of 'image'.[10]

At most the language of reflection in the early chapters of Genesis instructs us how we are to read the rest of the canon though not necessarily what we will find there. Reflection is a hermeneutical principle more than a substantive theological one. We read the Scriptures with the expectation that there will be reflections along the way, some of which may appear natural while others appear as surprising divine intrusions into the story. It is not the only methodological constraint in reading the canon, but without this constraint we will miss much of what follows.

The methodological point simply amounts to this – a mirror reflects. A distorted or broken mirror also reflects, but in a distorted or broken fashion. Paying attention to reflections in the canon is to pay attention to the way in which the human narrative reflects the larger divine narrative. But the human narrative is broken and sometimes distorted. When we read the narrative, we should pay attention to the reflections, though care must be paid because sometimes they distort the divine realities to which they point. In other words the methodological constraint is negative as well as positive. Our attention should be drawn not only to the abundance of ways God is reflected in human creatures, but also to the diverse ways those reflections distort divine realities. Light is refracted in any number of ways across the canon. Paying

---

[10] This is not to say that there are not significant background clues to the use of ṣelem 'ĕlōhîm in Gen. 1:26–27. Rather it is to say that there is a paucity of uses across the canon that would inform the use of the ṣelem 'ĕlōhîm in Gen. 1. Chapter 3 below spells this out at greater length. For a very fine-grained analysis of the background clues to ṣelem 'ĕlōhîm see Beckerleg 2009.

attention to the manner in which the reflections illuminate the meaning of creation and the manner in which they distort their Creator are two interpretative guidelines.

The methodological commitments of the *imago Dei* are manifested in how we read the canon and also how we read ourselves. The language of the *imago Dei* draws attention away from ontological accounts of human identity towards theological accounts. Human identity is in view rather than human nature.[11] Accounts of human nature wrestle with the mind–body relationship, with the shape of human faculties, with the relationship of the will to the emotions, and so on. Theological accounts of human nature wrestle with these issues in the context of a wider theological framework. By contrast accounts of human identity wrestle with the issues of the meaning of human existence. Affirming that the language of *imago Dei* is a claim about human identity is to say that the *imago Dei* is part of the wider theological framework in which human meaning is embedded.

The opening chapters of Genesis for example want us to ask questions such as the following: Wherein do we find meaning for our lives? What grants our actions significance? What is important about other people? When we ask these sorts of questions, we are paying attention to human identity rather than human nature (in chapter 2 below I explain the difference between these concepts).[12]

Questions about human identity push our explorations towards certain kinds of questions in the context of our own lives. Why are images important in our lives? Why do we pay attention to what others think about us? What is the role of power, money or reputation? Why do these social dynamics matter?

The portrait of Simone points us in the right methodological direction. Her image is well crafted with certain goals in view. Her (un) reality is constituted by what other people think about her. Her power has little to do with physical strength or political will or with substantive human attributes. Understanding the nexus of social realities that surround her 'image', we realize Simone may be ontologically thin while yet having enormous social significance and weight.

---

[11] I take this to be Kelsey's (2006: 139–158) point in reverse when he argues that the *imago Dei* is substantially insignificant in providing details of a Christian account of human nature.

[12] Theological anthropology has tended to think more about human nature than human identity, and as a result has misinterpreted the *imago Dei* as constituted by a set of human attributes. Undoubtedly much can be said and should be said about human attributes, but not on the basis of the limited exegetical grounds of the *imago Dei*.

An account of human identity is not in the first instance descriptive of constituent attributes but rather thinks of meaning in social contexts – one of which is the social context of divine–human relationships. These are the lived contexts of perceptions about what matters and why. And in turn these lived contexts derive from some important ways in which they have been created and called to live. The canonical account I am seeking to describe is an account about how life is lived as reflections of God and as reflected in our communal contexts. These accounts are not concerned with a static observation of things out there. They are accounts that begin with the fundamental shape of the God–human relationship as Creator and creature, as image maker and image bearer. Thinking about human attributes as reflections of divine attributes has a role to play but it is a derivative project to the one pursued here, and makes more sense inside the wider theological framework of the image maker to image bearer relationship. That wider theological framework is more nearly in view at the outset of the canon than the narrower one of distinctive attribute reflections.

This is important to establish because it restrains the pretensions to develop a full-blown philosophical anthropology out of a relatively scant amount of conceptual resources in the canon. It also helps to keep in focus the inextricable relationship across the canon between God and humankind, between Creator and creature, between image maker and image bearer. In large measure we are striving to let the Scriptures ask the questions before we leap ahead and offer the answers. If the *imago Dei* is a methodological postulate at the outset of the canon, it is appropriate to offer some methodological comments about the canon. In what follows, 'canon' will refer to those books that have formed the identity of the Christian church, because of the conviction that God has authorized these texts as his own. That authorization is rooted in the claim that God has authored the Scriptures in conjunction with a multitude of human authors. His authorship has not diminished the human production of these texts, but neither has the full humanity of these texts diminished their divine authorship. The canon is a single work of God with diverse parts. It is not a single work of any human author, but divine authorization of the canon entails that it be read as a single work whose unity is complex. It must be read as a totality in order to understand it.[13]

---

[13] I am here combining two arguments made by Wolterstorff (2004: 217–232). The authorization argument is made most fully in his *Divine Discourse* (1995).

The church has also confessed that the God who has authorized these texts as his own is one God and three persons. The canon is a single work of God, but is a complex single work. The mystery of the Trinity simply makes more complex the divine authorization of the canon. The unity of the canon is grounded in its divine authorization, but this unity must reflect the triunity of the divine author as well. This requires conceptual resources rich enough to capture a triple-agency discourse. Human analogies are limited but may help. The collaboration in most film-making is integral to the final 'product'. It is not primarily the work of one agent but of many. It would be wrongheaded to suppose that the different 'strands' of a film could be unwound into its distinct parts, each of which stands on its own. Academy awards may be given for distinct parts of the final production, but this hides rather than illuminates the truly collaborative nature of film-making. So it is with large works of architecture. Castles and cathedrals are enormous collaborative projects that nonetheless are single works on a massive scale. Rooms that appear as disjointed from each other may nonetheless fit into a pattern when the castle is viewed as a whole.[14]

The interpretative consequence of the canon reflecting the triunity of its divine author is that knowing the meaning of any text is a function of knowing the meaning of every text. As we read the canon, the historical conditions under which the multiple authors and editors produced the books of Scripture are not to be privileged above the triunity of its divine authorization. There are no mechanical guidelines here. Keeping the whole in view while we read the parts and the parts while we read the whole is vital.

If the canon should be read from whole to parts and from parts to whole, then it may be helpful to lean on dramatic notions of unity and diversity to provide further conceptual resources. The canon may be compared to a theological drama.[15] There is a plot that progresses. There are ironic twists and turns to the plot. Characters are thicker than they might at first appear. Speeches take many different forms: monologues, conflict-filled conversations, poetic whimsy, proverbial counsel, even silent non-verbal forms of communication. So Scripture is historical writing, wisdom literature, prophetic challenge and apocalyptic visions all rolled up into one grand 'epic'. Each book of the Scriptures is conscious in its role as a distinct 'act'

---

[14] Bartholomew and Goheen 2004a.
[15] Vanhoozer 2005.

in the drama. A reader paying attention to the forest as well as the trees will see this.[16]

That 'forest' can be framed in any number of ways. Calling it a 'single work' simply draws attention to the claim that there is a meaningful way to talk about the unity of the canon. It does not yet fill out what the nature of the 'work' is. Consonant with much work in biblical scholarship in the last half century, it is important to note that a significant thread across the whole canon is the enactment of covenants between God and his people.[17] From this lens each book has some sense of being party to historical and covenantal relationships between YHWH and his people. The new covenant is new only if there are old covenants. The complex relationships between the old and new covenants animates most of the books of the New Testament. That there is an archetypal fulfilment of the covenants in the life, death and resurrection of Jesus points at the interpretative relationship between him and all of the covenants prior to his appearance. The forest and the trees matter very much in this case.[18]

The books of the Bible also consciously relate events, themes and characters that expound the nature of God's dealings with his people and his people's dealings with him. Marital themes of fidelity and infidelity are played out across most parts of the canon because of the conviction that marriage was an institutional reflection of the relationship between God and his people.[19] This is not to argue for a peculiar way of 'interpreting' any part of Scripture. It is the admonition to interpret books of the Bible as connected to the drama of Creator and creature. A plot line 'holds' the books together, though that plot line is at times overwhelmingly complex.[20]

Quite obviously the drama metaphor cannot capture the full breadth of the whole to the parts and the parts to the whole of the canon. The individual books in the canon do not appear as one chronologically ordered drama. And one should be careful not to subsume the diverse genres represented in the canon neatly under the one genre umbrella of a dramatic narrative. This would be to privilege the whole while diminishing the parts, or at least some of the parts. Yet the drama

[16] Lints 1993.
[17] For a helpful introduction to the hermeneutical significance of covenants in Scripture see Horton 2006.
[18] Cf. Vos 1948 for a thoughtful analysis of the covenantal threads that tie the Bible together as a whole and their interconnections.
[19] Cf. Hugenberger 1994 for an extended argument to this effect.
[20] A helpful essay that both defends and clarifies this claim at greater length is Bartholomew and Goheen 2004b.

metaphor oft mentioned in contemporary discussions of theological interpretations of Scripture serves a useful function in restraining the more dominant impulse to privilege the parts over the whole.[21] Striving to keep the metaphor itself thick enough to account for the interesting diversity across the canon therefore remains important.

Yet there is no 'one size fits all' template of diversity for all the structures of our lives, nor for the canon of Scripture.[22] Some forms of diversity are trivial and some have eternal significance. Some are appropriate and morally commendable, while others distort the divine character and the triune reflections of that character in the created order.

The modern construct of democracy has given us a much richer discourse of diversity, but it has also unleashed a rhetoric of pluralism that too quickly flattens out differences, and thereby masks the many kinds of differences we encounter. Our cultural context can also submerge the diversely appropriate ways we might deal with different kinds of diversity. The language of diversity is different from the language of pluralism. The dominant cultural rhetoric of pluralism has too often run roughshod over more subtle distinctions of diversities. So to some the language of pluralism signals the unmitigated disaster of postmodern democratic culture. To others the language of pluralism protects all that we should cherish in a modern democracy. But this truncates the language of diversity into two and only two perspectives. Often times the heated rhetoric of our public discourse does not allow us to find the virtues of diversity we might hold in common, the vices of other forms of diversity about which we are needlessly divided and a host of other forms of diversity about which we will have to learn to deal with differently.[23]

Let me suggest that the differences that matter in the canon are those that reflect the conceptually interesting differences in the Trinity. That is to say, the Trinity exercises control over the differences in Scripture. This is the principle of hermeneutical absorption alluded to earlier.[24]

---

[21] Notable examples in addition to Vanhoozer 2005 of theological works employing the dramatic motif include von Balthasar 1988, Horton 2002 and Wright 1992.

[22] Lints 2013.

[23] Lints 2011.

[24] Being 'absorbed' is a term borrowed from many within the so-called Yale School (Hans Frei and George Lindbeck most particularly). It was once called the New Yale School, but since all the major players have retired or passed on and the framework is no longer the cohesive vision at Yale Divinity School it seems appropriate to refer to it as the Old Yale School. The fullest articulation of the absorption principle can be found in Frei 1974. The clearest summary of the principle can be found in Marshall 1990: 69–102.

Throughout the biblical witness large constructs illuminate the complex relationships in which we are embedded. One of the first to appear on the pages of Scripture has to do with humans themselves. Genesis 1 narrates the primal creation not of one individual, but of two diverse people who nonetheless are united by a relationship into 'one flesh'. Although different, they belong to each other. Male and female are created as beings who offer something the other does not have. They find satisfaction in the intimacy of their union, which is richer by virtue of their differences. We might say the idea of 'person' from the beginning of Scripture is a 'being involved in the relationship of unity and diversity'. In some important sense people find their meaning only in relation to another person who is different from them.[25] The words instituting marriage in Genesis 2 function not merely to cement a social contract between consenting parties, but rather as a deeply theological claim on their reflected identity. Marriage is a significant recognition of this unity in diversity across the canon.

It has become increasingly obvious that Scripture, accompanied by a corresponding suspicion about older notions of 'individualism', presents humans as essentially 'social'. The pendulum is swinging in our public conscience towards notions of personhood rooted in communities and away from Cartesian 'solitary minds'.[26] Christians ought to celebrate this swinging of the pendulum in part because it opens the door to recognizing more clearly the nature of our unity and diversity as created human beings framed by the Scriptures. If the cultural pendulum were to swing too far in this direction, individuals would cease to be anything above their relationships. That is not likely to happen anytime soon in the West, though there are cultures outside the West and small literary communities in the West where this has begun to happen. In our land of 'What's in it for me?' rank individualism still shows no signs of losing its traction.[27]

Across the canon is another significant relationship for humans, that of creature to Creator. If God is ontologically prior to us, as the Bible affirms, then he is also the source of all that we mean by 'person'. Consequently there is a relationship to God as 'other' that captures the identity of human personhood. It is appropriate to say that human identity is constituted in relationship to God. It is also true to say, asymmetrically, that God's identity is not rooted in his relation to

[25] Volf 1996.
[26] W. Barrett 1986. Putnam's (2001) work charts this pendulum swing.
[27] The now classic Putnam 2001 amply testifies the enduring strength of individualism in contemporary consumer cultures.

humanity. His existence is rooted in the triune relationships that exist prior to and thus apart from creation. God's permanence as 'three persons in eternal communion with each other' grounds his independence from human personhood. By contrast, the transitory character of human personhood grounds its dependence in the triune persons.

The *imago Dei* captures this transitory identity – as an image is contingent upon the object for its identity, so the *imago Dei* is contingent upon God for its identity. Conversely the Scriptures use the language of 'idolatry' when this dependence upon God is subverted in religiously significant ways. The idol may be ontologically vacuous but is still incredibly powerful. Its power lies in the transformation of the divine image bearer into the image of the idol. People, who are created as divine image bearers, are also capable of reflecting the created order. Thus humans may be said to have a reflective identity. In some sense they find meaning outside themselves by virtue of what they reflect.

The language of 'image' argues for a dependence upon an 'original'.[28] The nature of 'dependence' is not manifest until something further is known about the image, the original and the relation between them. The earliest account of the *imago Dei* (Gen. 1:26–27) is notoriously silent about the character of that concept as such.[29] The witness of the Scriptures as canon serves as a touchstone for these matters and to which Christian theological enquiry is indebted.[30] The shape of the canonical story suggests that the overriding relation of the image (humans) to the original (triune God) is that of worship, honour, completion and satisfaction, and conversely suggests the subverting of that relationship of image to original is that of perversion, corruption, consumption and possession.[31]

It is a relational dynamic that connects image (person) to original (God) but it is also a relationship of worship or honour that depicts this connection. From the beginning to the end of redemptive history the image is constituted by its (dis)honouring of God. The image

[28] Some of what follows finds its genesis in the work of Meredith G. Kline (1980), and then in turn from Henri Blocher (1984).

[29] By most reckoning, the language of 'image' (*ṣelem*) in the Gen. 1 account is rooted in the ancient construct of a concrete form representing an invisible deity. See the related articles under 'Image', in *NIDNTT* 2, 284–293.

[30] Grenz (2001: 267–303) provides a paradigmatic hermeneutical discussion of the *imago Dei* – moving from Genesis to the remainder of the canon and then returning from the end to the beginning.

[31] C. Plantinga (1995: 10) argues that 'sin' is conceptually messy. So idolatry is never merely 'one sort of practice'. Rather it is a large umbrella of concepts, all of which subvert the original relationship between image and original.

(humankind) finds its *telos* (purpose) in the honouring relationship to the original (God the Creator). This is true at both the beginning and the end of the canon.

Human identity is rooted in what it reflects.[32] That reflection will be strong or fragile as a function of this 'reflected relationship'. The reflection of fleeting material goods such as money or power will be tenuous and transitory. The reflection of the living and loving God will be enriching and enduring. The dynamics of human identity, however, are similar in both instances. Humans gain an identity in the social network of reflections in which they are embedded and upon which they set their hearts. In this respect, as Leora Batnitzky comments, 'God and idolatry are codependent conceptually and in the lives of the faithful.'[33] Identity and idolatry are intertwined. This draws our attention to the conceptual resources and restraints that the canon itself places on this dynamic. We turn to the beginning of that project in the next chapter.

---

[32] Beale's (2008: 16) work on idolatry has paid particular attention to the exegetical basis of this conceptual claim. He takes his initial clues from Isaiah's witness to idolatry and summarizes the claim, 'what you revere you will resemble'. He has painstakingly followed the textual clues about the role of idolatry in Israel's sojourn after their entrance into the Promised Land. I am indebted to many of his exegetical insights, particularly in the major prophets, as chapter 5 below bears out.

[33] Batnitzky 2000: 11.

Chapter Two

A strange bridge: connecting the image and the idol

Idolatry . . . is no game of ideas, no conceptual matter, but a
question of power: not whose it is, but to which one submits.

(Rumscheidt 1999: 96)[1]

Getting started on the wrong foot: creation and image

At the heart of the opening chapters of Genesis lies the claim that
God is the Creator of all that is. He creates by speaking all that exists
into being. There are no signs of warfare in the background nor do
there appear to be any conflicts into which God enters and that are
resolved by divine creation.[2] God is not one among many creators,
nor is he acting on behalf of other gods when he creates. His sovereign
act of speaking creation into existence separates him from all that is
created. He alone is the uncreated one.[3] All else is dependent upon

---

[1] Cited from an article commenting on Karl Barth's charge of idolatry against Nazi
socialism.

[2] This is a controversial claim given the language of Gen. 1:2 with the affirmation that
the earth was 'without form and void' (*tōhû wābōhû*). It is often asserted that the presence
of evil as represented by the earth's formlessness and void is an indication of a primeval
conflict between good and evil, mirroring the conflict imagery of other ANE creation
myths. See Westermann 1984: 73–84 for the review of this argument. However, the absence
of 'conflict imagery' from Gen. 1:1 – 2:3 is striking if in fact a grand cosmological battle
is taking place. Re-examining Gen. 1:2 in the light of its immediate context and its
canonical context suggests no conflict is in view. *Wābōhû* occurs only three times in all of
the Hebrew Scriptures (Gen. 1:2; Jer. 4:23; Isa. 34:11), and in every case it appears together
with *tōhû* and appears as a repetition of emphasis. *Tōhû* makes sixteen solo appearances
in the Old Testament, and by all accounts appears to refer simply to a lack of something
positive. This would argue that in Gen. 1:2 the account of creation is framed by the claim
that anything creation possesses positively God has made it thus. Cf. Samuelson 1992:
15–17. See Clifford 1994 for an extended argument against the conflict model.

[3] Assman (1997: 8) refers to the uniqueness of the biblical distinction of Creator
and creation as 'the most fundamental of all distinctions' for the Judeo-Christian
tradition. The absoluteness of this distinction stands in contrast to the Egyptian and
Mesopotamian blurring of the distinction such that Creator and creation stand on a
relatively equal ontological footing in their creation stories.

God.[4] Divine speaking frames the originating divine activity of creation as a purposeful event. This significance is nothing less than the reflection of God's character in creation. In this regard creation is invested with the 'echo' of God's glory.[5]

From the vantage point of the creation everything that exists beside God is dependent upon him for its significance. This is the remarkable conviction of the prologue to the entirety of the canon.[6] God has chosen to be reflected in creation and thereby granted to everything meaning and value, the pinnacle of which is his reflection in humans.[7] Whatever else the *imago Dei* might mean, there can be little doubt that it stands as paradigmatic of all creation in its calling to reflect or mirror God. It is an exhilarating and exalting description, intended to signify the privilege of imaging God. It is also a humbling description, reminding humankind that it is not divine, but merely an image of the Creator.[8]

It is a common conviction in contemporary theories of religious language that the human authors of Scripture endlessly search for apt metaphors for God from their own world of experience.[9] While this is undoubtedly true at some level, it masks an underlying premise that ought to be resisted. That premise is simply that human experience lacks essential categories of analogy and so analogies must be created by human authors as they search for ways to speak about God. The church's conviction across the ages, however, has been that God has put the categories of analogy into creation as the means of understanding him. He creates the contexts that are reflective of his character and aims. The canonical authors are persuaded that marriage, for example, is an apt metaphor for

---

[4] This is underscored by noticing that the Hebrew verb 'to create' (*bārā'*) is uniquely an action of God. It serves to distinguish this divine activity from every other creaturely power or ability.

[5] Some of the general framework that follows finds its genesis in the work of Kline (1980) and in turn from Blocher (1984).

[6] See I. Hart 1995: 315–336 for the beginnings of this argument linking the themes of Gen. 1 to the rest of the canon.

[7] The prepositions in Gen. 1:26 '*in* our image' and '*after* our likeness' contrast with the absence of the prepositions in 2 Cor. 4:4 and Col. 1:15, where Jesus '*is* the image'.

[8] Clines (1998: 447–497) argues that the primary purpose of the 'image' language is to exalt humankind and only secondarily to humble it. He does, however, not shy away from seeing both aspects in the Gen. 1 account of the *imago Dei*. Brueggemann (1982: 29–31) also notes the dialectical consequences of the language of *ṣelem* (image) – to exalt and humble.

[9] McFague 1982.

divine fidelity because marriage is ordained by God for this very purpose.[10]

A wider biblical-theological argument would point at the divinely ordained categories of understanding emerging from the 'reflective' nature of human identity. God so constitutes human beings with the purpose of reflecting him in the created order that it is essential to their identity that this reflection 'fill the earth' (Gen. 1:28). The categories of their understanding of their Creator grow naturally from the reflective nature of their identity and the reflective nature of their reflection in the rest of the created order.

In the history of theological discussion the nature of the *imago Dei* has in large measure been parsed in metaphysical or moral ways, namely in terms of human faculties of rationality, spirituality or morality as the essential elements of human identity created in God's image. More generically, the opening chapters of Genesis have been thought to assert a complex cosmological system with attendant ontological implications about existence and causal contingency. Everything that has existence is caused to exist by God. But how exactly are humans distinct from everything else that is created? Do humans have a different kind of existence or a different set of capacities? The faculties of mind, will and spirit were put into this nexus of cosmology and creation by theologians across the centuries. Theological debates about human identity often revolved around which of these faculties were essential to humans as distinct from the rest of the created order.[11] The metaphysics of these human faculties were of central theological importance in the patristic debates about sin and salvation as well.[12]

The focus on human faculties that distinguished humankind from the animals and reflected the divine being led to cosmological musings during the Middle Ages that pertained abstractly to the causal relation between God and creation more generally. What was the nature of causal dependence? What was the difference between God's necessary existence and creation's contingent existence? What was the difference between God's knowledge and human knowledge if he did not have a body and was therefore not causally dependent upon the senses for

[10] It is hard to make sense of the recent controversy over definitions of marriage apart from this controversy about divinely ordained categories of understanding in creation. Helpful Old Testament background to this claim, though not in the context of the recent marriage controversies, is Ortlund 1996.

[11] Cf. Berkhof 1939; Hodge 1986; Strong 1886.

[12] McGuckin 2004 is instructive for certain theologians of the early church, while Wilken 2005 is important as regards the intellectual traditions of the early church.

'information'? In each of these queries was the struggle to find a larger theoretical framework to understand Creator and creation. These debates were (and are) important, but often obscured the original intent of the 'doctrine' of creation in the early chapters of Genesis. A wide literature has emerged offering sophisticated accounts of scientific cosmology that are sympathetic to a religious understanding of human nature, and that have not sought to pit the Bible against science, nor to prove the Bible from science.[13] This has helped to distinguish two tasks, which nonetheless have some overlap: the exegetical and the cosmological. Metaphysics is not the primary concern of the Genesis account, though undoubtedly ontological consequences are manifest in Genesis, into which theologians and philosophers have justifiably enquired. But if Genesis 1 is a text connected to Israel's existence, then the account ought not to be seen as primarily an abstract affirmation of *creatio ex nihilo* (creation out of nothing) but 'rather the emergence of a stable community in a benevolent and life-sustaining order'.[14]

Human identity and human nature

It is important to distinguish the questions of human identity and of human nature. Questions of identity have to do with meaning. What is the meaning of human life? Wherein do our securities and insecurities lie? What are appropriate goals towards which human striving is aimed? What is the meaning of human flourishing? The questions of human nature have to do with a description of human faculties and capacities. What is the relationship of the human body to the human person? What is the most adequate metaphysical description of personhood? How does human biology relate to human psychology?

Undoubtedly there is overlap in these two diverse clusters of questions. However, realizing that they are different sorts of questions will enable us to know what sorts of evidence might count towards answering the different questions. Understanding our human DNA is part of the story about how humans are related to the animal kingdom. But DNA does not necessarily answer questions about the meaning of life. By contrast, saying something about justice and mercy would not necessarily answer questions about mind–body issues.

[13] Helpful summaries of some of the most important findings of natural science that lend towards a religious orientation are Collins 2006 and McGrath 2009.
[14] Levenson 1988: 12.

The issues of the canon are predominantly questions of human identity rather than of human nature. There are restraints in the canon for any full-blown theory of human nature, but the description of human capacities in metaphysically and scientifically appropriate ways is not the animating concern of Scripture. The Scriptures are permeated throughout by the questions of meaning.

Too often theological treatments of the *imago Dei* have oriented themselves towards accounts of human nature and less towards human identity. Theologians have every right to be interested in questions of human nature, but the unfortunate consequence is that they have therefore made the construct of the *imago Dei* bear more conceptual weight than it was intended to bear. The context of the primary occurrences of the *imago Dei* in Genesis 1 – 9 strongly argues against construing the *imago Dei* as a grand metaphysical construct. If anything, the context demands a certain theological humility regarding this.

The 'image' language in Genesis 1 – 9 occurs in the contexts of a longer covenantal argument about Israel's relationship to YHWH as Creator, and thus an account of the *imago Dei* should not be turned into a generic account of natural human attributes.[15] In the context of the covenantal argument the central concern was the meaning of Israel's existence and their security from the threats surrounding them as well as those within their own midst. These are the matters of human identity, not in an abstract sense but in the concrete relationship to YHWH. What does it mean to find security and significance in YHWH? What are the dangers to that security and significance?

These questions provide the clue that the language of *imago Dei* underwrites a positive construal of meaning and a warning to the dangers and threats to that security and significance. In the canon the closest conceptual counterpart to the *imago Dei* are graven images. Idolatry provides the wider canonical context for the *imago Dei* as that which most centrally threatens the security and significance of the covenantal relationship between Creator and creature, between Redeemer and redeemed, between Christ and his people. Paradoxically, the idol-maker is the theological opposite of the image bearer. But it is true both exegetically and theologically that bearing the image of God and crafting graven images are two sides of the same conceptual coin. The Creator has made human creatures whose

---

[15] This is the argument of chapters 3 and 4 below.

identity enables them to move seamlessly from worshipping the living God to bowing before other gods.

Human identity is illuminated in the covenantal relationship of bearing the image of God, and is corrupted by exchanging him for graven images. The one made in the image of God 'exchanged the glory of the immortal God for images resembling humans and birds and animals' (Rom. 1:23). This 'exchange' highlights the remarkable similarity and absolute difference of imaging God and imaging the idols. The actions are virtually the same but the objects that receive the action are fundamentally different. The root metaphor for Israel's relationship to God and to the idols is that of marital relationships.[16] As husband and wife are forbidden to have sexual relations with any other partner, so Israel is forbidden from worshipping any but their true Bridegroom.

Listening to the canon will aid us in refraining from constructing elaborate theological or philosophical anthropologies out of the *imago Dei*. It will also likewise remind us how dangerous is the subversion and perversion wreaked upon us by our own graven images. The task before us is much more limited than theologians have traditionally supposed, but the result is much more important.

Finding security in YHWH is rooted in the covenantal claim that he is the Creator of Israel (and of the whole created order), whose identity is grounded in a peculiar relationship to him. That peculiar relationship arises because humans represent YHWH in a way that nothing else in the created order represents him. The promises of YHWH's presence among his people underscores this peculiar relationship. He is everywhere present in creation, but is uniquely present in his covenantal relationships. He is redemptively present in the exodus event. He is present in judgment during the periods of exile. He is present in ways that bring forgiveness in the Holy of Holies in the temple. The narrative of that divine presence corresponds to the persistent narrative of dangers that threaten Israel's well-being in the world.[17]

This narrative of redemptive history is conceptually rich, but we should be careful to discern the nature of the constructs used. The primary constructs in this study are *imago Dei* and 'idolatry'. Construed as constructs inside a narrative, they point generally at some kind of representation. The image represents or reflects that of

[16] Halbertal 1992.
[17] Cf. Beale 2004.

which it is an image. The idol represents the gods to which it points.[18] Representation is itself not always straightforward. Ambassadors are representatives of their governments. Flags represent a country's identity. A painted portrait represents the person of which the painting is made. Some forms of representation are natural; others are a result of mere conventions.[19] Some evoke a powerful emotional response, as when a memento of a dead person kindles strong memories of that person. Other forms of representation go virtually unnoticed because of sheer repetition, as when words refer to objects. Reading the marks (letters) on a page often produces an unconscious formation of a mental image of an object. Our minds can move to the consideration of the object without noticing the convention of representation inherent in the written word.

It is the biblical narratives that determine the kinds of representation packed into the concepts of 'image' and 'idol'; and it is important to note at this point that both constructs involve some kind of representation. Clearly the *imago Dei* connotes a positive and 'idolatry' a negative representation. The opposition to idolatry throughout the canon does not suppose that representation of every sort is negative, but simply that the unique kind of representation in idolatry is aberrant.

When Michelangelo painted God on the ceiling of the Sistine Chapel, no one supposed that God was there. The image was different from that which it represented. But there were nonetheless theological critics of Michelangelo's project because it mistakenly supposed that God had material representations. The critics argued that God could not be pictured as if he were a creature. As a Jewish commentator notes of the critics, 'the material representation of God would lead to the conception that he is a material being'.[20]

However, the canon does occasionally suppose that God has a material image (Num. 12:8; Ezek. 1:26; 8:3). Isaiah speaks of seeing 'the Lord sitting upon a throne' (Isa. 6:1). Ezekiel writes of the

---

[18] In the ANE there is good evidence to demonstrate that the physical idol included both representation and manifestation in the mind of the idol-maker. The idol represented the god and also made that god manifest. Beckerleg (2009) argues that the ancients had no problem conceiving the idol as both an 'image' and as 'true god' even after it was carved as an image into stone or wood. The idol represented the god and was the god manifest in concrete form.

[19] Peirce (1991: 141–144) writes of three kinds of representation: similarity, causality and convention. I am adapting Peirce's analysis into a different context, but find his categories helpful in distinguishing the different ways objects or words can point at other objects.

[20] Halbertal 1992: 260. Eire (1986) also hears this sort of criticism frequently in the writings of the Protestant Reformers.

appearance of God in human form on the throne. YHWH is recorded as saying to Moses, 'you cannot see my face, for man shall not see me and live' (Exod. 33:20). God is said to have a 'right hand', 'ears to hear' and 'feet' to walk.[21] Each of these in turn points to the unexpected conclusion that God communicates that those human forms may appropriately be ascribed to him. Undoubtedly these do not imply straightforwardly that God has a body, and must be viewed as consistent with the common claim in the canon that he cannot be seen or touched, because he is not a material being.[22] The Creator is not to be confused with the creation. However, the chasm between Creator and creature is not so great that God cannot bridge it. God 'enters' into the story of creation in a host of unexpected ways – speaking, acting and making his presence manifest, all within the confines of the created order. Any account of the relationship of the Creator and the creature that makes the chasm either too great or too small does an injustice to the mysteries and tensions of the canon.

Part of the reality of the chasm has to do with the nature and direction of worship and desire. A mistaken conception of God as a material being is but a small part of the negative connotations of idolatry. Believing something false about God is dangerous, but not nearly as dangerous as worshipping something other than him. 'The boundary between idol worshippers and monotheists is not the metaphysical picture of the world, but the method of relating to it, the method of worship.'[23] False representations pull the creature away from the Creator. They exert an influence over the creature in unforeseen ways. They tug at the human heart and distract it.

The image gains its ontological weight from what it represents. It is ontologically 'thin' in this sense, derived from the original. Without an original there is no image. It is not conversely true, however, to say that without an image there is no original. In canonical contexts the image is a thin or thick reality dependent upon the object of its desire. If its object of desire is the living God, then it is filled with life. If there is

---

[21] The use of these phrases throughout the Psalms is numerous: Pss 16:11; 17:7; 18:35; 20:6; 21:8; 44:3; 45:4; 60:5; 74:11; 78:54; 80:15; 89:13; 97:1; 110:1; 118:15; 137:5; 139:10.

[22] Beale (2004: 20) in his biblical theology of idolatry notes of these rare occurrences, 'These appear to be legitimate exceptions to the rule, especially since these are living appearances sovereignly initiated by God himself and not lifeless images in an artistic way to depict the parts of the creation, as long as these representations were not thought to represent God.'

[23] Halbertal 1992: 5. Halbertal goes on to argue that idolatry is related to marital metaphors of infidelity, and only in the Middle Ages does it begin to connote 'wrong belief' or heresy.

only one true and living God, there is nowhere else to find life, and so if the object of greatest desire is anything else save YHWH, there is a corresponding thinning out of the image. The idol is doubly 'thin' in this respect, since it depends upon the gods it represents who themselves have no life. The constructs of idol and image overlap and both are conceptually codependent upon the nature of God. The idol and the image both take their clue for meaning from outside themselves, either in reverence or in rebellion to the only true and living God.

The story of the image and the idol is not one of bare existence. It is not simply whether the image can exist independently of the original or whether there is a metaphysical description of image as a human person. The story is about the meaning of life rather than the metaphysics of life. The image finds its flourishing in its relationship to the original. Creatures find their satisfaction in the God who made them. The idol represents both a false fulfilment and a perversion or corruption of the creature. The canon goes to great lengths to narrate the tug in human hearts between the living God and the idols who pull them away from the living God. Idols are dangerous in the same way that outside love interests are dangerous to a marriage. Adulterous liaisons inevitably pull the marriage apart at the seams. As with adultery, so idolatry is about both wrong beliefs (e.g. a belief about where satisfaction can be found) but more importantly corrupted desires (e.g. the desire to get gratification on whatever terms are necessary).[24] All idolatry involves error in belief to some extent, if the belief in question is that some creature has a worth enjoyed only by the Creator.[25] If there is only one God, there is only one object worthy of worship and adoration.[26] Monotheism and monolatry go hand in hand. The worship of one God (monolatry) is a necessary consequence of the belief that only one God exists (monotheism).

It is appropriate to use the language of addiction in reference to idolatries. The idol becomes a nasty taskmaster whose power seems almost limitless to the idolater, comparable to the way an addict is enslaved to alcohol or drugs or sex or shopping. The addict

[24] Even 'good' desires may become idolatrous when they become ends in themselves rather than means pointing to a greater end. Keller (2009: 24) writes, 'Making an idol out of love may mean allowing the lover to exploit and abuse you.'

[25] Helm 1995: 420.

[26] Seeskin (1995: 15) writes, 'If there is only one God, there is only one thing in the universe worthy of worship; everything else is part of the created order and subject to the will of God. In fact, the division between God and creation is so decisive that not only are heavenly bodies, mortal creatures and sea monsters not divine, they cannot even serve as images of the divine.'

experiences powerlessness in the face of the addiction. Addictions are complex, progressive and often disabling.[27] But addictions are entered into voluntarily and often without much forethought. They do not begin with raging compulsion. But somehow mysteriously desire turns into compulsion and addicts lose a sense of their former identity. What drives the addiction is a longing for satisfaction. This desire for fulfilment runs deep in the human heart. Satisfaction, however, is not to be had simply anywhere or with anyone. It is part of the hardwiring of the human heart that satisfaction will be found in that which is finally good and true and beautiful, namely God. The error of idolatry was in the longing for gods that 'are no gods' (Jer. 2:11).

Idols are not the sorts of things one ordinarily considers in the abstract, whether it is reasonable to believe in them or not. Looking for good reasons to believe in idols is a category mistake. We are attracted to idols not on rational grounds but rather as means to gratify desires. We believe in idols because we want to, even as an alcoholic is attracted to alcohol because he wants it. There is rational consideration only in the very vaguest of senses.

Idolatry ironically became a powerful tool in the hands of secular thinkers over the last two centuries.[28] It sustained an enduring critique that religion itself is mistaken because it concerns matters of the heart rather than of belief systems. As I will argue later, the secular Enlightenment of the eighteenth and nineteenth centuries exploited this characteristic of idolatry to claim that religion itself was not rational.[29] Since God is beyond any evidence, Feuerbach and Nietzsche both assumed that the whole of the religious project must be a form of idolatry – of creating a god to suit one's own interests.[30] Marx replaced the true and living God with the essence of humanity in his natural state of labour. On this scheme money was the worship of an alien god at the expense of man's true nature. Discovering the motives

---

[27] Cf. C. Plantinga (1995) for a lengthy description of the correspondence between sin and addiction. This correspondence argues not for denying human responsibility but rather for a thicker theological description of sin than is found in the popular literature. The following comparison of idolatry and addiction is deeply influenced by Plantinga's treatment.

[28] Batnitzky 2000.

[29] See chapter 8 below.

[30] Feuerbach 1957; Nietzsche 1987. Karl Barth wrote an introductory preface to Feuerbach's *The Essence of Christianity* (1957: xi) and tellingly says, 'His principal aim was to change the friends of God into the friends of man, believers into thinkers, worshippers into workers, candidates for the other world into students of this world, Christians, who on their own confession are half-animal and half-angel into men – whole men.'

for religious belief then became the mode of argument to uncover the religious illusion. Uncovering those motives proved a powerful alternative to the project of having to prove that God did not exist. If it could be shown that religious belief arose because of psychological need or economic oppression, then religious belief could be swept away much more quickly and efficiently.

The fundamental flaw in this line of reasoning is by now well rehearsed. If all claims about God, including the claim that he does not exist, derive from ulterior motives, then atheism is susceptible to the critique of ulterior motives as well. This critique itself, though, is instructive when viewed in the light of the canon. In the canon it is not those outside Israel whose sins are particularly exposed by the framework of idolatry. Rather it is Israel themselves, those who are peculiarly religious, who are prone to a thick and destructive idolatry. When Christians recognize this propensity in themselves, it leverages the power of the gospel against the power of idols.[31] It also creates an inbuilt tendency not to believe too strongly in oneself. In fact it teaches us to distrust our natural tendency to demonize others and downplay the seriousness of our own idols.

Taking one's idols more seriously requires understanding how meaning is created and human identity is constituted. It requires more than mere suspicion of motives. Idolatry is unmasked not by a sheer unmitigated self-criticism. Idolatry requires a light that illuminates its true character. Throughout the canon that 'light' is none other than the true and living God. This is the reason why we must resist those traditions that supposed God was beyond all comprehension, and thus that all theology must be merely negative.[32] If there is no positive task for the knowledge of God to perform and therefore no genuine knowledge of him, then one's best hope is the muting of idols rather than their replacement. But the canon strongly argues that the only defence against idolatry is God himself. There must be a window through which he can be known, in order that a light may shine back upon the idols, unmasking them for what they are. It is only in comparison to the one true living God that the idols are manifested as mere pretenders.

---

[31] Keller 2009.

[32] Most often these traditions were grounded in the claim that God's transcendence is always dangerously compromised by any positive construal of his nature and being. See Williams 2000 for a helpful introduction to the tradition of 'negative theology' in the early church. In a recent collection of essays, Davies and Turner (2002) explore the insights of the apophatic traditions without fully embracing absolute transcendence.

The notion of a light shining or reflecting the identity of God into and against the idols is the function of the *imago Dei* rightly considered. The identity of God illuminates the identity of the *imago Dei*, which in turn illuminates the true identity of the idols. Put differently, images will reflect. The key question of the Scriptures is, what will images reflect? Will the image of God (humankind) image God? It seems a simple question. Will the image of God find his or her identity in the reflection of God?

Image bearers are not intrinsically idolatrous though they are doxologically fragile. The *imago Dei* of Genesis 1:27 is the striking counterexample to the universal ban on images in worship.[33] This 'image' is not an object of corrupted desires, yet the image bearer is strikingly prone to chase after graven images. The image bearer finds purpose in worship, quite obviously not as an object of worship but as the one whose significance and security are defined by the reflection and representation of God. Graven images by contrast draw these image bearers away from their doxological relationship to God and thereby virtually replace the Creator with the created. The surprise at the end of the story of the graven images is the appearance of the perfect image. The divine entrance into the very likeness of our humanity in Jesus Christ is the great irony in the narrative arc that runs from the creation of the image to the corruption by the graven images and finally to the revelation of the perfect image. It is the narrative arc of this story of image to idol and back again to image that is told across the rest of this work. By drawing attention to this biblical-theological thread woven across the canon we will more fully appreciate the depth and the richness and the surprise in the manner in which redemption plays out in the great epic of Scripture. To the beginning of the epic we turn in the next chapter.

---

[33] Blocher (1984) argues that the Second Commandment, 'You shall not make any graven images', is intended to protect the sanctity of the original image of Gen. 1:26 as much as it is intended to protect the worship of the one and only true God.

Chapter Three

The liturgy of creation in the cosmic temple

> The point of creation is not the production of matter out of nothing, but rather the emergence of a stable community in a benevolent and life-sustaining order.
>
> (Levenson 1988: 12)

The first table as prologue

The theological consequences of the *imago Dei* claim in Genesis 1:26 are to be found in the immediate context of Genesis 1, in the larger context of the Pentateuch and also in the context of the biblical canon considered as a whole. Those interpretive horizons suggest that the significance of the 'image of God' ought to be found in the context of creation, in connection to the prohibition of making graven images and finally in the new creation in Christ, who is the perfect Image. To see the sweep of this theological construct across the breadth of the canon is to begin to appreciate its fuller significance for contemporary discussions of human identity.

There are two accounts of creation in Genesis. The 'first table' runs from Genesis 1:1 to 2:3. The 'second table' runs from Genesis 2:4 to the end of chapter 3.[1] The two accounts of creation in Genesis 1 – 3

---

[1] Part of the interpretive controversy regarding the relationship of the two tables concerns where the first table ends and the second begins. In particular should 2:4 be divided or not? A sizeable number of commentators in the twentieth century have placed all of v. 4 in the second table. The *tôlĕdôt* formula ('These are the generations of') at the beginning of v. 4 is viewed by the majority as a colophon marking out the genealogical material to follow. The primary grounds are semantic. Everywhere else the formula *tôlĕdôt* is used it is connected only to material that follows. See Hamilton 1990 for a summary and defence of this viewpoint. See also Wenham 1987, Levenson 1988 and Stordalen 2000. By contrast the others have supposed that 2:4 ought to be divided, the first half of the verse (with its *tôlĕdôt* formula) summarizes the first table and forms an inclusio with 1:1. The latter half of v. 4 ('In the day that the LORD God made the earth and the heavens') introduces the material to follow. In its favour is the awkward transition of the *tôlĕdôt* formula of v. 4 if taken as a whole. The first half of the verse uses the word order 'the heavens and the earth', while the latter half of the verse switches the order and omits the definite pronouns 'the earth and the heavens'.

have been a point of great discussion over the last hundred years.[2] The older historical-critical orthodoxy supposed that Genesis 1:1 – 2:3 had been written by an anonymous writer associated with the Priestly school of the post-exilic period. Supposedly the account was written to protect the sacred rituals surrounding the temple, most especially the ritual calendar grounded in the 'days' of Genesis 1. The second account of creation (Gen. 2:4 – 3:24) allegedly came from an amalgam of sources concerned to protect neither the priestly functions nor the ritual calendar, but edited to preserve a democratizing trend as against the authority of the priests.

But if we turn attention to the tables considered first in relation to each other, and to the remainder of the canon, it is apparent that the two accounts do not stand in awkward relation one to the other, each offering a competing account of Israel's origins for political purposes. Asking the standard historical-critical question in reverse – namely how might these two accounts be connected, as opposed to how they might be in conflict – leaves one with different impressions of the two tables. If those early chapters belong together, a clue to their connection may be the larger role they play in the Pentateuchal material – and in particular with laying foundations constitutive of Israel's origins and the nation's unique relationship to God. The older pre-critical intuition that Genesis belongs fundamentally to Israel's canon as a means to interpret the nation's place in the wider history of the Gentile nations is ironically an integral part of the newer (post-critical) readings of Genesis as well. These both in turn suppose that the primeval history of Genesis 1 – 11 belongs in Israel's canon to signify Israel's place in that primeval history, a history that encompasses all of the created order.[3] It is intended to signify Israel's purpose in relation to the created order and to the Creator.

Prior to jettisoning the older historical-critical orthodoxy entirely, at least one important insight about the first table ought to be salvaged. This is the intuition that the first table manifests a peculiar liturgical shape, illustrative of a community concerned about temple matters. In what follows I will argue, though briefly, that the first

---

(Cont.) There is no parallel in any of the other *tôlĕdôt* formula for this. See van Wolde 1996 for a defence of this view, along with Brueggemann 1974 and Beckerleg 2009.

[2] Westermann (1992) and Hamilton (1990) each offer helpful summary treatments of this historical-critical interpretative tradition of the two tables of Gen. 1 – 3 in the twentieth century.

[3] McBride 2000: 3–41.

table is a liturgical preamble to the rest of Israel's story, and in part the liturgy of the first table illuminates one of its central constructs, namely the *imago Dei*. To use different language, Genesis 1 is a prologue to a story of how and why Israel were to worship their God in contrast to the worship of the gods of the nations surrounding them. The onus on worshipping God is grounded in part by the claim that humanity has been created as the image of God. This argues for seeing the covenantal arrangement between Israel and their God as a covenant of worship, as well as connecting the constructs of imaging God and worshipping idols as mirror images of the same liturgical impulse.

Research in the middle part of the twentieth century illuminated the peculiar literary shape of covenant treaties in the ANE.[4] This in turn shed significant light upon the treaty-like character of much Pentateuchal material, including the preamble to the treaty in the first chapter of Genesis.[5] Taking this treaty concern seriously, the first account (Gen. 1:1 – 2:3) offers a prologue to the story of Israel as a covenant people, and the second account (Gen. 2:4b – 3:24) is the first story (the first of the *tôlĕdôt*s) in that covenant history.[6] Neither table is intended as a secular history of Israel, but their history is told in such a fashion as to make a claim upon Israel's loyalties to YHWH above all. It is a sacred history that neither floats above history nor is contained fully in that history. It is not simply a story about beginnings, but rather the framework within which all other stories are placed. In this regard the first table serves as an overarching preamble to the rest of the Pentateuch. It is a covenantal preamble that defines the ultimate destiny of Israel.

Most recent commentators have taken the final form of Genesis to be structurally built around the oft-repeated Hebrew phrase *tôlĕdôt* (these are the generations) found at the beginning of major sections

[4] Mendenhall (1955), the most influential of Old Testament scholars emphasizing ancient treaty covenants, noticed the similarity between Israelite covenant texts and a group of Hittite state treaties, the so-called suzerainty treaties. He argued that the structure of Israel's covenant with YHWH found its origin in ANE treaties of the Hittites, most particularly in their historical prologues.

[5] An older work that offers a fine summary of this 'covenantal treaty' framework as a fruitful lens through which to view Pentateuchal material is Kline 1963.

[6] Gunkel (1910) effectively framed the discussion of Genesis throughout the twentieth century as a portrayal of a 'saga'. Also see von Rad 1972. Gunkel's most important interpreter until the mid-century accepted the language of 'saga' as an appropriate designation but asked how it fit with the language of 'faith' that so permeated the account. At mid-century Vos (1948) suggested this (saga/faith) was the relationship between a covenant people and their peculiar covenant history.

of narrative material or genealogies.[7] On this score the first table appears as a distinctive literary unit from that which follows, for it has no *tôlĕdôt*.[8] The absence of the *tôlĕdôt* phrase in the first table suggests that Genesis 1 is not simply the first of the 'stories' of Israel's prehistory recorded in Genesis, nor is it intended as a genealogy of the heavens and the earth. The signal of 2:4 introduces the change of focus from the first to the second table in the inversion of 'heavens and the earth' at the beginning of verse 4 to the 'earth and the heavens' at the end of the verse. This inversion is unique in the canon. Whether 2:4a with its *tôlĕdôt* formula belongs to the first or second table, it signals a change of focus from above to below in the transition from the first to the second table.[9]

Further, the prose in the first chapter seems at odds with the style of the other material in Genesis, and it does not have anything approaching genealogically structured material. Most especially its rhythmic organization suggests its author or editor intended this material for a unique purpose in the book as a whole. The central characters in the biblical drama are introduced in the first table, but not in customary fashion.[10] We do not come to know Adam or Eve in Genesis 1, but simply humankind as male and female. God is not revealed by name, but rather portrayed simply in stark contrast to everything else. He creates. Everything else is created. He blesses the creation. The created order is blessed. He speaks. The created order is silent. For these reasons the first table ought not to be construed as

---

[7] The phrase is found in Gen. 2:4; 5:1; 6:9; 10:1; 11:10; 11:27; 25:19; and 36:1. It is also found, interestingly, in Exod. 1:6 at the beginning of the 'Moses Story'. Mathews (1996) offers a helpful summary of approaches to the *tôlĕdôt* structure of Genesis.

[8] Cassuto (1961–4: 45–50) offers interesting internal evidence to consider the *tôlĕdôt* of Gen. 2:4 as belonging to the second table rather than the first. He notes that the paragraph descriptive of the seventh day is replete with repetitions or multiples of seven. This pattern falls out altogether if 2:4 is counted as belonging to the preceding verses.

[9] Taking 2:4a as part of the first table may not be obvious, but it safeguards this literary signal, often missing in the traditions that take all of 2:4 to belong to the second table. For a spirited defence of the unity of 2:4, but that sees it as a literary signal of transition, see Cassuto 1961–4. He (1961–4: 99) summarizes the purpose of 2:4, 'It serves to connect the narrative of the first section to that of the second; and its meaning is; [*sic*] These – these events described in the previous portion – constituted the history of the heavens and the earth, when they were created that, when the Lord God made them, and now I shall tell you in detail what happened at the conclusion of this Divine work.'

[10] The recent work by Horton (2002) exploits the metaphor of 'drama' as an illuminating theme for a theological description of the covenant relationship between God and his people. In drawing attention to the metaphor of drama I am intending to mark out Gen. 1 as an introduction to the drama rather than as a chapter in the drama itself.

the first story in the Bible, but rather as an interpretative lens through which the rest of the stories will be viewed.

The two accounts of creation are not at odds with each other, if we understand Genesis 1 to be a prologue or preamble rather than one of the 'stories' of Genesis.[11] The two tables of creation do use different names for God and this has long been the central evidence allegedly driving interpreters to the conclusion that these are conflicting and competing accounts of creation. The fact that the simple name for God (Elohim, God as all-powerful) is used in the first table and his compound name (Elohim-YHWH, God who is almighty and is also the Lord of Israel) is used in the second is itself a sign of the canonical relation between the two tables. The first table tells us in liturgical form that God is the absolute one who causes all that is to come into existence. The Word(s) of God fills creation. God is the one in whom all else finds meaning. A most powerful expression of his prerogative to grant significance is found in the echoes of the creation account in YHWH's deliverance of Israel at Sinai.[12] YHWH brought Israel out of Egypt in order that they would worship him, the purpose for which he had created humankind in the first place. The Ten Words (i.e. the Ten Commandments) form the framework around which Israel's relationship to YHWH was to be structured, even as the word of God originally gave creation its (liturgical) structure. The Exodus narratives echo many of the themes of the creation prologue of Genesis 1, which has led many commentators to suppose that Sinai is a kind of 'second act' in the drama of creation.

God as almighty (Elohim) is the subject of every verb in the first table. This marks him out as the sovereign Creator and serves as the subtext to the first table: God alone creates.[13] In the second table Adam

[11] So Cross (1998: 83) remarks, 'The [first] creation account is a prologue attached to an epic account of the call of the fathers, the victory of the Divine Warrior in the exodus and conquest, and the creation of the covenantal political order at Sinai.'

[12] The repetition of the themes of creation at Sinai are an indication that this founding event in Israel's history is itself interpreted (at least in part) as a 'new creation'. This is manifest in the grounds offered for the second commandment in Exod. 20:4 prohibiting the making of graven images, namely by appeal to 'heaven above, or that is in the earth beneath, or that is in the water under the earth'. The grounds call to mind the initial theatre of creation as framed by Gen. 1. Interestingly these are virtually the same grounds offered in support of the fourth commandment to honour the Sabbath, namely calling to mind Gen. 1 but now noting the initial rhythm of creation – work and then rest.

[13] There has rightly been scepticism recently about viewing Gen. 1:1 as a claim about the beginning of time. The Hebrew word translated 'In the beginning' (*bĕrē'šît*) is an ambiguously tensed word with respect to time. Unfortunately this has led some in turn to cast doubt on the deeply entrenched theological belief in *creatio ex nihilo*, on the

and Eve are granted narrative status as actors and speakers on the stage of history alongside God. 'History' begins, so to speak, in the second table.[14] And therefore God as almighty (Elohim) of the first table is manifest as God the almighty, Lord of Israel (Elohim-YHWH) in the second table. God relates specifically to human actions and thereby the author uses the personal name of Israel's God (YHWH) who is also the uncreated Creator of the universe (Elohim).[15]

The first table draws attention to the actions 'from above', while clearly the verbs of the second table focus on those within the primeval garden. The climactic nature of the Sabbath in Genesis 2:1–3 stands in stark juxtaposition to the climactic character of the 'fall' in Genesis 3:1–6. After the former, there is satisfaction. After the latter, there is shame. The former portends a completeness, whereas the latter portrays a brokenness. The shalom of the Sabbath is shattered in the conflict of the fall. But it must be remembered that the Sabbath principle endures from the beginning to the end of the canon, and is not thereby obliterated by human rebellion. In this the first table casts a shadow over the rest of the canon, revealing the *telos* of the canon, namely that the created order, and humankind in particular, finds its meaning in the worship and reflection of God. This is ultimately the principle to which the Sabbath points.

The liturgy of creation

The densely structured character of Genesis 1:1 – 2:3 is by now a well-rehearsed theme in the commentary literature.[16] The central activity in the first table is divine speech, and that speaking is portrayed

grounds that Genesis nowhere has in view what actually happened at the beginning of time. However, the overwhelming impression of Gen. 1 is that God alone creates and that he creates everything. These two convictions by themselves would strongly incline one to see *creatio ex nihilo* as a straightforward consequence of the first table of creation. One should also keep in view that the three-tiered creation (heaven above, seas below and earth in the middle) may seem mythologically antiquated, but to the Hebrew mind it was a primary way to signify all that is. In other words if God created the heavens and the seas and the earth, then he created all that is. It is this claim that Augustine (1991) referred to as *creatio ex nihilo*.

[14] Vos 1948. The second table is not a straightforward historical narrative by any means. This is evident in the sacramental signs and symbols serving largely typological functions at the outset of the canon. The tree of life, the tree of the knowledge of good and evil and the serpent each in turn resist being read on strictly theological terms.

[15] McBride 2000: 8.

[16] Anderson (1977: 151) remarks, 'the story [of Gen. 1] is a meticulously wrought composition in which form and content are indissolubly linked'. See also Brown 1993 for another detailed analysis of the 'dense structure' of the first table.

THE LITURGY OF CREATION

with exquisite literary skill. The record of the divine speaking is highly stylized: more nearly like a hymn than a philosophical, scientific or historical lecture. The testimony to God's creative acts of speaking creation into existence is filled with repetition and overlap.[17] Though without the ordinary rhythms and parallelisms of Hebrew poetry, the account portrayed is a lyric account of events.[18] It has a 'liturgical bent' to it noticeable by its style as well as its substance.[19]

The hymnlike character of the first table of Genesis is most evident in the 'pairing' of the days, marking out the different stanzas of creation.[20] Each 'day' of creation is matched with a corresponding day, with one noticeable exception – day seven. Days four, five and six each in turn refer back respectively to days one, two and three. Day seven alone has no 'pair' and quite evidently serves as the climactic stanza in the hymn. The overtly heptadic structure of the first table is itself testimony to viewing one of the days as climactic. How, then, are the days paired? And in what consists the uniqueness of the day that has no pair? The obvious answers have to do with God's actions portrayed on days one to six and the lack of any divine action or work on day seven. Further, the specific divine actions on days one to six illuminates their significance in the light of the liturgical concerns of the first table. Consider the following.

Day four refers to the sun and moon, which are said to govern the day and the night. The 'day and night' of day four point back to day

[17] The most prominent example of repetition noticed by early Judaism was the tenfold repetition of 'then God said' (*wayyōmer 'ĕlōhîm*), corresponding to the ten commandments of the Decalogue. See Blocher 1984 and McBride 2000: 10.

[18] So Weinfeld (1981: 510) writes, 'The recurring formulas: "And he saw that it was good", "and it was evening and it was morning", are a type of refrain which imparts to the chapter a liturgical character.'

[19] It is no accident that Israel viewed Gen. 1 as a primary ground for viewing their week as well as their general calendar in liturgical terms. So e.g. the Exod. 20 account of the Decalogue lists the grounds for keeping the Sabbath day as reflecting God's rest in Gen. 1. The routine of commandments six and one is also echoed in Sabbath years (when debts were to be cancelled, Deut. 15) and in jubilee years (seven sevens of years, Lev. 25).

[20] The 'days' of creation have tempted many commentators to see a chronology being defended explicitly in the first table. Even some commentators not concerned with the chronological debates about creationism versus evolution in the early chapters of Genesis nonetheless have argued for a chronological pattern to creation as narrative. So van Wolde (1996) interprets Gen. 1:1 – 2:4a as a story with temporal sequence. God does certain things before he does other things. Though van Wolde does not argue for a strict chronology in the story of creation, she does see the unit narratively structured and therefore sequenced in chronological fashion. I am arguing rather that the literary unit is not narrative in tone, but lyric or hymnic. This ought not to suggest that the first table has no historical or chronological consequences, but simply that it is not a narrative account whose central structure is chronology.

one, where the hymn of creation began its tribute to God. On day one God as Elohim issues the divine command 'Let there be light.' That command is followed by his separating the light from the darkness, calling the light 'day' and the darkness 'night'. On day four God creates the heavenly bodies that rule the day and the night. The language of 'rule' is military in background and suggests a kind of conquest or subjugation. However, there appears no resistance or opposition on the part of those realms to be 'ruled' by the heavenly bodies. It is more accurate to say that by God's sovereign word a positive order is placed upon the created realms of day and night.[21] In this regard the account had in view that day four would illuminate the sacred order to which day and night always point. Time itself is filled with divine purpose and structure if the relation of days one and four is treated seriously.

The principle by which day five was paired with day two is different from days one or four but again illustrates the overarching purposes of the first table. The animals mentioned in day five are to 'fill' the sea and sky, realms originally mentioned on day two. The governing relationship of day four to day one has been replaced by a filling relationship of day five and day two. Day two is 'filled' by day five. The language of filling is a distinctive command of God here by virtue of his ownership of the whole created order.[22] He commands the filling of the seas and skies because they belong to him. This world is a proverbial divine temple in this regard. The created order is sacred space precisely because God owns and fills it.[23] This language is echoed in later canonical contexts when the glory of the Lord is said to fill the temple, as well as in contexts of covenantal declarations when God promises his appointed representative that his descendants will fill the earth.[24]

[21] This is in part Levenson's (1988) argument, in which he claims Gen. 1 is centrally about God's sustaining order in the face of potential chaos. Levenson leaves open the possibility that there is a primeval chaos suggested in Gen. 1:2 with its language of *tōhû wābōhû*, 'formless and void'. However, I take Gen. 1:2 to imply rather a lack of any structure (positive or negative) prior to God's command. For further argument to this effect see Samuelson 1992.
[22] The imperatives *pĕrû* (be fruitful), *rĕbû* (increase) and *mil'û* (fill) in Gen. 1:22 are repeated together three other times in Gen. 1:28; 9:1 and 9:7.
[23] There are analogies in other ANE contexts where gods involved in creation are said to fill the creation as they fill their temples. See Levenson 1984: 139–158.
[24] On the connection between filling and temple see 2 Chr. 5:11 – 6:3. On the connection between filling and covenant see Gen. 17:6 and 35:11. It is interesting to note that in both of these contexts (temple and covenant) there are royal overtones. The building of the temple is presided over by the king (Solomon) and the promise of descendants to fill the earth is also accompanied by the promise that some of those descendants will be kings.

The governing and filling relationships are combined in the pairing of day six with day three. On day six God speaks the land animals, including humankind, into existence. The animals and humankind are to 'fill' the earth. However, an additional imperative falls upon humankind to govern the rest of living creatures who fill the created order. Again the language of 'governing' carries military connotations, but without any resistance in view it must point to the greater reality already hinted at, namely that humans rule after the 'order' God has established for his creation. The military vitality of the language suggests this is no ordinary command, but one to be carried out with the utmost care. So day six fills day three, while it is also true that humans serve, at the end of the creative activity of God, as his royal representative called to be diligent in protecting the sacred order established. In humankind, then, comes the consummate connection between filling and governing.[25]

It is also evident that creation is narrated from the top down. The realm of the heavens appears first, then the more immediate skies and seas, and finally the land spaces. Each realm is prepared for its filling by God's act of dividing, first the day from the night, then the waters above from below, and finally the land from the seas. Each realm in turn is filled in descending order, from the sun and moon created as hosts of the heavens, to the birds and fish as hosts of the sky and seas, and then finally to the land animals, including humankind as the hosts of the earth. This twofold descent (separation followed by creation of the hosts), by which creation is outfitted from top to bottom in the first table, is neatly summarized in Genesis 2:1, 'Thus the heavens and the earth were finished, and all the host of them.'[26]

The completion of the realms and their hosts awaits, however, a yet greater 'completion' on the seventh day, and in particular the cessation of divine labour and the enjoyment of the divine Creator in his work.[27]

---

[25] It is also noticeable that day three leads naturally into the second half of the sextuplet of creating days. On day three there is the divine creation not only of dry land, but also the first hints of life with the creation of vegetation.

[26] Both Westermann (1984) and McBride (2000) draw considerable attention to the manner in which creation occurs from the top down. Notice also the summary of creation in Neh. 9:6: 'You are the LORD, you alone. You have made heaven, the heaven of heavens, with all their host, the earth and all that is on it, the seas and all that is in them; and you preserve all of them; and the host of heaven worships you.' The principle of 'filling' here, as in Gen. 2:1, is expressed in terms of there being 'hosts' of heaven.

[27] Most commentators have seen that God's 'rest' was not to recuperate from fatigue, but to celebrate the completion of his creation of a royal dwelling, to enjoy, as it were,

There are no verbs of divine activity on this day, nor does the day of divine rest have the analogous temporal boundaries of the previous days.[28] Day seven appears without 'evening and morning', suggesting that the language of 'day' (*yôm*) is itself not used as a temporal indexical but rather as a teleological signal in the first table. Creation has a purpose and that purpose is signalled by the climactic day seven. God grants meaning to everything – time as well as space.[29]

There are other structural clues to the hymnlike character of Genesis 1. Day four, which stands in the numerical middle of the heptadic structure of seven days, points back to the first day (by virtue of the governing of the day/night) and also points ahead to the seventh day in the command that the sun and moon are to 'serve as signs to mark seasons and days and years' – an obvious reference to the 'Sabbath' principle associated with Israel's feast days.

The hymnlike first table has seven stanzas, though only six of them close with the refrain 'and there was evening and morning'. Justifiably, these refrains have been viewed as the interpretative backbone of the passage. However, there are other 'groupings of seven' independent of the seven days. Seven times the author uses the phrase 'and it was so'. Seven times there is the recognition that 'God saw it was good'. The first verse consists of seven words; the second, of fourteen. This remarkable calculation of numbers is no accident of a very careful author or hymn writer.[30]

his own enthronement. The temple imagery is extended in the second table in Genesis with God's command to Adam to protect the temple-garden from the presence of evil. See Vos 1948, Kline 2006 and Weinfeld 1981.

[28] The significance of the Sabbath in the first table of Genesis echoes throughout the remainder of the canon. Suffice it to say here that the Sabbath appears as a principle linking creation, redemption and consummation. The argument of Heb. 4 makes this clear. See Dumbrell 1989: 137–156 and Bacchiocchi 1998.

[29] Westermann (1984: 90) writes of day seven, 'the celebration of the holy gives unity to the whole'.

[30] Cassuto (1961–4: 12) notes of these numerical patterns, 'The structure of this section is based on a system of numerical harmony. Not only is the number seven fundamental to its main theme, but it also serves to determine many of its details. Both to the Israelites and to the Gentiles, in the East and also in the West – but especially in the East – it was the number of perfection and the basis of ordered arrangement.' Levenson (1988: 68) remarks on Cassuto's argument, 'What do the heptadic structures [in Gen. 1] prove? For Cassuto, it proves the compositional homogeneity of the passage: no text with so many heptads subtly threaded in from beginning to end could possibly have been stitched together from preexistent documents. This is a point that scholars would be well advised to concede to Cassuto.'

The house that God built

The summary so far. There are remarkable signals in the first table pointing towards an intensive theological liturgy of creation. The account powerfully reminds the reader that creation is 'built' for worship. The liturgical shape of the first table points to the conclusion that the created order as portrayed in Genesis 1 is a kind of temple in which the glory of God is reflected and the divine presence rests. In this respect creation is a theatre for the worship of God, though he is not merely a stage presence, but intends to be present throughout the created order. The created order is temple-like because it is filled with the presence of the divine King, the purpose for which God built this temple in the first instance.

This, then, draws attention to the temple imagery as appropriately applied to creation. Some archaeological evidence suggests that temples in the ANE were often constructed in terms of 'seven'.[31] Temples were considered sacred space, and seven, as the sacred number, was appropriately applied to the architecture of the temple. So it is also true in later Israelite history that temple building and the number seven were connected.[32] Solomon's dedication of the temple occurs during the seven-day Festival of Tabernacles during the seventh month. After the exile in Babylon, Ezra likewise mentions the Festival of Tabernacles in connection with the reconstruction of the altar of the temple (Ezra 3:1–6). Sacred time and space were interrelated.

If this was so, then it is safe to say that Genesis expounds the creation of the cosmos as an ordered creation after the manner of the sacred rhythm of time. Seven signified a completion or perfection appropriate to the divine work of creation. It also signified that a sacred space had thereby been made. The cosmos is a kind of temple by virtue of being intentionally ordered as sacred space. That sacredness is clear with the use of the number seven. And therein is the connection between the cosmos as intentionally ordered and the cosmos as a temple. In the mind of the composer of the liturgy of creation this must not have been an accidental connection.

The analogy between temple and cosmos is also indicated by the prominence of new creation themes in the building of the new (second) temple after the exile. This rebuilding of the temple is explicitly called

---

[31] Fisher 1963: 34–41. Fisher argues that Ugaritic temples built in honour of Baal in 2100 BC were constructed intentionally in sections of seven.
[32] Levenson 1988: 79–80.

an act of new creation in Isaiah 65:17–19.[33] The announcement that God is creating a new heaven and new earth in the building of a new temple underscores the Israelite contention that cosmos and temple are signs of each other. The similarities between this passage and Genesis 1 therefore are in all likelihood no mere coincidence.

A final thread of evidence linking creation and temple is the overlap between Genesis 1 and the Exodus 39 – 40 account of the building of the tabernacle.[34] The pattern of completing, being filled with God's presence or glory, and blessing as a sign of the holiness of the space are remarkably similar in the creation of the cosmos in Genesis 1 and the creation of the tabernacle in Exodus 39 – 40. Similarly both accounts (building the world, building the tabernacle) recount how God brought about an environment in which he could find 'rest'. Sabbath and sanctuary were intertwined, representing an exaltation and regal repose, a moment free of anxiety. The Sabbath climax in the liturgy of creation echoes in the continual injunctions to observe the Sabbath in imitation of God while the tabernacle is being constructed. Cosmos and temple were connected at this point in the mind of the canon.

It is not incidental that temple themes were noticed in early Jewish interpretations of Genesis, exemplified by the early Jewish commentator Philo of Alexandria:

> The highest and in the truest sense, the holy, temple of God is, as we must believe, the whole universe, having for its sanctuary the most sacred part of all existence, even heaven, for its votive ornaments the stars, for its priests, the angels who are servitors to His powers.[35]

Genesis 1 celebrates the reality that God has built a temple in which he will reside, though he will never be contained by that temple. The governing language of days four and six strongly suggests a sacred and royal temple is in view. The filling language of days five and six points towards the ever-increasing glory of God throughout the royal temple. God's presence inextricably grows and fills everything, and is to be reflected by all living creatures.

---

[33] These verses read, 'For behold, I create new heavens and a new earth; / and the former things shall not be remembered or come into mind. / But be glad and rejoice for ever in that which I create; / for behold, I create Jerusalem a rejoicing, and her people a joy. / I will rejoice in Jerusalem, and be glad in my people; / no more shall be heard in it the sound of weeping and the cry of distress.'
[34] Levenson 1984: 280–282.
[35] McBride 2000: 15.

God enters the temple to rest (Ps. 132), not because he is tired from building this temple, but quite clearly because he is uniquely satisfied with the building. The Sabbath declaration in the Decalogue (Exod. 20) looks to God's 'rest' as the justification not for relaxation but for worship. Worship is a temple activity because God's works are the evidence of the worthiness of honouring or worshipping him. After Exodus 20 in the context of the Sinai wilderness, Israel understand that the presence of God is uniquely located in the tabernacle as a sign of the divine presence throughout the whole tabernacle of the created order.

The building of the tabernacle (Exod. 39) typologically mirrors the building of the created order (Gen. 1).[36] Both describe the completion of the task commanded by God. In Exodus 39 Moses is the agent through whom those commands come. In Genesis 1 obviously God issues the commands directly. In both accounts, of the tabernacle and of the created order, there is an inspection and final approval or blessing as well as a setting apart of both for sacred purposes. The Sabbath rest is the appropriate conclusion to both building projects. The tabernacle is a symbol of the whole universe with one critical difference – the presence of evil. The divine presence is available not immediately but mediately because of sin. In Genesis 1 the Sabbath rest is undisturbed by evil. In the building of the tabernacle Israel are warned to keep their distance because of the evil in their midst.[37] The presence of God, still ubiquitous throughout the created order, nonetheless takes on a redemptive and judgmental aspect in the building of the tabernacle. Herein is the tension between the universal and particular presence of God. His universal presence throughout creation has been and continues to be affirmed from Genesis 1 forward. His particular presence, as revealed to Israel through Moses, neither undermines nor is to be equated with that universal presence. The manner in which Israel as God's chosen people are nonetheless to be a 'blessing to the whole world' still remains to be explained, as at the time of Israel's wilderness experience narrated in the book of Exodus.

---

[36] Weinfeld 1981: 503.

[37] The analogy with Israel's experience at Sinai is instructive. God's presence is uniquely located on the mountain. There is a waiting period prior to Moses' ascent of the mountain. The people are strictly warned not to come close lest they see God and die. The dark cloud and quaking thunder signal the coming of God onto the mountain. Even on the summit his appointed mediator, Moses, is hidden in the cleft of the rock so that he does not directly see God. All of this points to the chasm between divine holiness and the unholiness present in and among the people. No such chasm of holiness is narrated in the first table of Gen. 1. On this see Cassuto 1967.

Returning now to Genesis 1, the analogy of God's creating acts and the project of building a temple help illuminate the place of the *imago Dei* on the sixth day. Genesis 1 is a hymn of royal temple construction.[38] The proverbial pictures on the temple walls are crafted on day six. The pictures serve as images of the builder who is also the governor or sovereign of the created order. The intertwining of the royal imagery with the priestly imagery throughout the Pentateuch is especially evident in the first table of Genesis. Humans are to be mediators or priests of the divine presence and also vice-regents in protecting that sacral presence. Humans created in the image of God are to rule all other living creatures in the diverse realms of the created order, after the manner of the divine rule. The vice-regents are still clearly subservient to Elohim, as the seventh day makes clear.

The temple-building activity of Genesis 1 serves the purpose of providing a throne room for the divine sovereign. The seventh day of the first table provides a picture of this implicit enthronement. Elohim as the sovereign builder of the temple 'rested' in the inner sanctum, the most holy place, as it would later be pictured in the tabernacle and then the temple. This day of divine rest is a consummation of all that has gone before because it inaugurates God's presence within the cosmic and created temple.[39]

Important exegetical issues remain in this complex account of creation. The point of the preceding reflections on Genesis 1 was to situate the immediate context of the *imago Dei* in order to connect it to the wider context of the Old Testament. The theologically rich role of the *imago Dei* ought first to be understood in its immediate context, and then to be related across the canon. The immediate textual horizon of the *imago Dei* on the 'sixth day' of the first table places an onus on any theological interpreter to understand the hymn of creation in which the sixth day occurs, before explaining the *imago Dei* in its own right.

[38] Hurwitz 1992.
[39] McBride 2000: 14.

Chapter Four

The image of God on the temple walls

The Old Testament has no interest in articulating an
autonomous or universal notion of humanness. Its
articulation of what it means to be human is characteristically
situated in its own Yahwistic covenantal, interactionist mode
of reality, so that humanness is always Yahwistic humanness,
or, we may say, Jewish humanness.

(Brueggemann 1997: 451)

Introduction

The canon begins the story of humankind by affirming the representation of the human creature in/as the Creator's image (*ṣelem*) and
likeness (*dĕmût*). There is little explicit commentary within the first
table about any wider meanings of 'image' and 'likeness' beyond that
which is straightforwardly on the surface of the text, namely that the
image reflects the original. Humankind in some manner reflects
the Creator. Left unsaid at this point in Genesis is the content of the
reflection, its character or the nature in which it occurs. This is not to
say that the context, both immediate and more distant across the
canon, does not speak to the issue, but rather that a nuanced construction of *ṣelem* and *dĕmût* ought not to be infused too immediately
at this point in Genesis and thereby their obvious and simple significance be missed.[1] Keeping things straightforward, Genesis 1 would
have us believe that humankind images their Creator and that this is
important to recognize.

The straightforward meaning of *ṣelem 'ĕlōhîm* (image of God)
argues against erecting a sophisticated philosophical anthropology
from the phrase at this point in the canon. The language of *ṣelem* is
itself an image, a word picture, not a technical and abstract term. It is
a metaphor taken from one realm of human experience and applied

---

[1] See Berkouwer 1962: 67–118 for further elaboration of this hermeneutical point.

to another. The relative paucity of appearances of this phrase in Scripture argues for restraint in building too much on its scant foundation.[2] A recent exegete noted the appropriateness of the Churchill-like phrase as applied to theology's enlarging of the construct beyond all imaginable bounds: 'There has never been so much made, with so little, by so many.'[3] In like manner, the dean of modern Old Testament commentators on Genesis, Claus Westermann, followed the intuitions of many contemporary exegetes when he wrote:

> Gen 1:26f. is not making a general and universally valid statement about the nature of humankind; if it were, then the Old Testament would have much more to say about this image and likeness. The fact is that it does not, and this has been noted on a number of occasions.[4]

And yet there can be little doubt that the phrase *ṣelem 'ĕlōhîm* is of unique importance in the first table of Genesis. It is applied to no other creative act of God aside from the act of creating humankind.[5] It breaks all of the previous patterns in God's creating work in this regard. In an account full of liturgical patterns this cannot be incidental. Though the act of creating humankind shares the same stanza with the creating of other land animals, the difference of language descriptive of each act is striking. The author of the liturgy of creation more nearly connects the divine act of creating the land animals with the preceding stanza and the creation of the birds and fish, each in turn reproducing 'according to their own kind' (*lĕmînēhû*; Gen. 1:21, 24–25).[6] When the time comes to describe the act of creating humankind, the author makes sure the reader understands the uniqueness of this act by omitting altogether the earlier repeated affirmation. The poetic parallelism in verse 27, when the author puts the proverbial flesh on the bones of the divine creation of humankind, is the clearest indicator that this act of creation is itself unparalleled in the rest of the liturgy of creation.

A second and equally compelling reason for taking the language of *ṣelem 'ĕlōhîm* as a uniquely important canonical construct is the

---

[2] From different quarters see both Clines 1998 and Kelsey 2006.
[3] Kutsko 1998: 55.
[4] Westermann 1984: 155.
[5] Clines (1998: 448) writes, 'The resemblance of humans to God is precisely what is not shared by anything else in creation and therefore its significance cannot be over exaggerated.'
[6] This was the language used of the vegetation also in Gen. 1:11–12.

enduring echoes of the liturgy of creation throughout the canon. The first table is just a mere thirty-four verses and yet its general framework as well as its key themes reoccur time and again in the canon.[7] This is noticeable in part by the recurring themes of 'creation and its hosts' in every major section of canonical material.[8] Likewise the recurrence of Sabbath themes across the canon argues for theological reckoning of the first table beyond its immediate context.[9] As well, the implicit temple theology of Genesis 1 finds echoes at critical locations throughout the Scriptures.[10] All of these suggest that attention ought to be paid to the echoes of the first table across the canon. So it suggests that the image and likeness of God, appearing so climactic in the first table, is very likely to echo in the background of other biblical texts, explicitly and implicitly.

Image and original

The language of 'image' is neither technical nor abstract. It is indeed an ordinary word picture intended to signify a central meaning about humankind in Genesis 1 and is unique to the canonical understanding of humankind. The conflict with other ANE texts of creation intrinsic to the liturgy of creation in Genesis 1 may provide cultural clues to the meaning of humankind's uniqueness as the *ṣelem 'ĕlōhîm*. As a prior act of interpretation, however, the core element of the word picture ought to be retrieved prior to entering the debates about its possible background contexts or later canonical usage.

'Image' or 'likeness' language argues for a dependence upon an original.[11] Whatever else may be said of an image, it must be clear that the image depends upon whatever it is an image of for its meaning. The nature of this dependence constrains us to keep both image and original in view when explicating the meaning of the image. Humans may possess many diverse qualities, but the emphasis of Genesis 1 is that whatever else may be true of them, they fundamentally image

[7] See Ridderbos 1957: 221–234.

[8] Sample references include the Pentateuch (Gen. 1; 14:22; Exod. 20:11; Deut. 5:8; 10:14), Wisdom (Pss 33:6–9; 90:2), Prophets (Isa. 40:26–27; Jer. 10:12–13; Amos 4:13), Gospels (Matt. 19:4; John 1:3), Epistles (Rom. 1:25; 1 Cor. 11:9; Col. 1:16), Revelation (4:11; 10:6).

[9] Sample references include the Pentateuch (Gen. 2:1–3; Exod. 16:29; 20:10–11; Lev. 25), History (2 Chr. 36:21; Neh. 9:14), Prophets (Isa. 56; Jer. 17; Ezek. 46), Gospels (Matt. 12; Mark 2; Luke 6; John 5), Epistles (Heb. 4), Revelation (21:1–4).

[10] Sample references include 1 Kgs 6; 2 Chr. 2 – 7; Ezra 3; Pss 11; 27; 65; Ezek. 40 – 43; Luke 19:45 – 20:18; John 1 – 2 ; Rev. 21 – 22.

[11] Some of what follows finds its genesis in Blocher 1984.

Elohim, their Creator. Care must then be exercised not to reduce all other aspects of humankind into the *imago Dei*, nor unnecessarily to broaden the domain over which the *imago Dei* extends. The *imago Dei* does not appear as a place marker for an otherwise long list of human traits and qualities. Nor does the *imago Dei* seem to be an umbrella under which many other concerns are placed. The *imago Dei* is the reminder that humans image God. It also suggests this is an important, and probably the most important, dimension of human existence, which the author of Genesis 1 desired to communicate in the liturgy of creation. But although the construct is central to Genesis 1, it is not exhaustive of what it means to be human. Genesis 1 certainly does not provide a list of human characteristics that are intended to fill out the account of the *imago Dei*.[12]

It is not without reason that theologians have historically asked what the underlying content or substance of the *imago Dei* consisted of as a means to understand more fully how humankind was to reflect their Creator. An image reflects by virtue of having certain characteristics. A mirror has a physical set of qualities by which it is possible to see reflections in the mirror. But we ought to remember that the question of the qualities inherent in humankind (the image bearer) is derivative from and secondary to the teleological claim of Genesis 1 that the *imago Dei* reflects God. Humankind reflects the divine being. The language of 'image' draws attention to this reflection of and relationship to God as the defining aspect of humankind in creation.

Though the reflection and relation are not identical, they are integrally related. What humans reflect is a function of how they relate to God. And in reverse the relationship between God and humans is manifest in the reflection. The substance of the reflection is the nature of the relation, and the evidence of the relation is the character of the reflection. The reflection draws attention to the reality that there is a unique relationship of humankind to their Creator, and further, this relationship is a defining relationship – it defines humankind in relationship to God. In turn that defining relationship is constituted by humankind being image bearers of God.

According to Genesis 1, humankind does not have the image of God, nor is it made in the image of God, but is itself the image of God. Genesis 1:26 reads, 'Let us make man as our image.' Though this may appear as a controversial translation or claim in the history of interpretation, it stands as the most straightforward reading of

[12] Ibid. 87.

Genesis 1:26.[13] Humankind is not fashioned after a pre-existing image of God, since God has no image. Rather humankind is created as the image or reflection of God himself. By contrast to ancient Caananite mythologies and their anthropomorphic deities, Genesis clearly asserts the transcendence of God from the physical order. Rather God creates a visible reflection of himself. The force then of adding that humankind is created in God's 'likeness' is that humans bear some resemblance to God but are not God. They are merely like him in some yet to be defined manner.

Humans are not exact replicas of God. They relate to him as their Creator, not as their equal. The context of the account in Genesis 1 is the creation of humankind as the image bearer of God, a reminder of the humbled state of humankind (only a creature) but also of their exalted state (uniquely created to image God). The substance of the relationship is defined by the manner in which the reflection of the original (God) in the image (humankind) manifests the God who created and who commanded. It is a relationship to a God who spoke and acted in peculiar ways. And it is those 'peculiar ways' that serve as the thread that holds the canon together and are thereby constitutive of those who bear the divine image. Bare notions of sociality will not sufficiently ground personhood in the canonical soil. It is not merely that humans are social creatures that constitute their purpose. It is a peculiar relationship to God that defines who they are. The canonical echoes of this are abundant. Israel are created for a peculiar relationship to YHWH. Christ enters history with a peculiar relationship to his Father. The church that goes out into the world goes because of a peculiar relationship to their trinitarian Redeemer. The story of redemption, whatever else it is, is the story of a peculiar relationship between God and humankind.

It is a relational dynamic that connects image (person) to original (God) but it is also centrally a relationship of worship or honour that depicts this connection. From the beginning to the end of redemptive history the image is called to honour God. The image (humankind) finds its *telos* in the honouring relationship to the original (God the Creator). This is true at both the beginning and the end of the canon. The story considered as a whole suggests that the overriding dimension of the creatures' relationship to their Creator is that of worship and honour. Conversely, the subverting of that relationship carries

---

[13] Clines (1998: 445) offers the most exhaustive and definitive treatment of the grammatical arguments in favour of this position.

the connotation of perversion, corruption, consumption and self-worship.[14] Humans are made in such a way as to yearn for something beyond themselves that grants them significance, most notably the God who made them as his image. God places humankind in his earthly sanctuary where all of life is sacred. All of life relates in some fundamental sense to God.

Signs of reflection

There are many hints in the immediate context of Genesis 1 that the theme of reflection is not incidental to the liturgy of creation. The emphasis upon light and illumination recurs throughout the first chapter of Genesis. God governs the temporal character of human existence with the presence of the sun and moon. They illuminate the earthly existence and serve as signs for 'seasons and festivals' – temporal spaces of enormous religious significance in Scripture (Gen. 1:14).

This cycle of Israel's weekly routine was marked off by the sun and moon climaxing in Sabbath practices. The echoes of this Sabbath pattern were also found in all of Israel's 'religious days'. Divine work was followed by divine satisfaction, which in turn framed Israel's work and their consequent worship. In this sense God's purposes are *reflected* in the illumination of human life by the sun and moon. The significance of worship is built into the very structure of creation with the presence of the sun and moon.[15] Whether one regards the heavenly bodies as themselves fulfilling a host of other natural functions, Genesis 1 clearly affirms their significance as marking out the sacred character of time and daily routine. This is no cosmological accident. Rather the liturgy of the temple of creation is composed in part with the harmonies of sun and moon in their sacred reminders.

While legislatively enacted at Sinai (Exod. 20), the Sabbath's ground is found in Genesis 2:1–4. The ground for the Sabbath (in the fourth commandment) clearly points to the intended reflection of divine work or rest in Israel's work or rest. The pattern of divine activity and satisfaction was to find its 'image' in humankind's activity and

---

[14] C. Plantinga (1995) argues that 'sin' is as conceptually interesting and diverse as righteousness is. It should not be construed as a thin construct. Sin is deep and requires us to pay attention carefully to its multiple faces.

[15] Van Wolde (1996: 19) notes that the heavenly bodies of Gen. 1 do not propagate themselves. In this manner they are viewed as permanent and thereby establish 'order and time on the earth'.

worship. The correspondence of divine and human work, and consequently of the reflection of YHWH in Israel's routines commanded at Sinai, was rooted in the Genesis 1 theology of reflection and illumination. As humankind reflected God, so the created order would be filled with the divine illumination.

Two thematic corollaries are highlighted in this canonical conviction – namely that of a reflecting relationship, and correspondingly that of light and illumination. The image bearer reflects God. The image bearer also illuminates the temple with that reflection. The mandate given to humans to multiply and fill creation in Genesis 1:28 is grounded in the prior claim that humans image their Creator. It is a double refraction in this regard, reflecting God and thereby illuminating creation with that reflection.

A reflected relationship

The unique character of the human reflection of Elohim is centred on the unique relationship constituted between him and his human creatures. God both speaks creation into being and is peculiarly involved in speaking to and with our human parents. He speaks as a person in relationship. He does not speak to the man and woman as equals but grants them a relationship by virtue of his words.

The divine–human conversation takes much greater shape in Genesis 2 – 3. The seeds of that communication and the peculiar relationship to which it gives rise are planted in Genesis 1. In that first chapter the only time God speaks in the first person occurs in the instance of creating the man and the woman. Three times on the sixth day the personal dynamic of God's speaking is emphasized with the use of the first person plural. Whatever else may be said of the use of these first person plurals (and more will be said below), they distinguish the speech of God with respect to humans and the rest of creation. The hint of intimacy is present in the first table in regard to this communicative act of creating humankind. God speaks personally when it comes to humans.

Elohim's words in the first table constitute speech acts of a performative nature.[16] The words accomplish that which is connoted in the words themselves. When God says, 'Let there be light,' the act of

---

[16] Wolterstorff (1995) defends the claim that God speaks not by virtue of having vocal cords, but rather by authorizing discourse as his own. In Gen. 1 God does not physically speak, but rather creates words (written and verbal) and in a peculiar way authorizes them as his own.

creating light is thereby enacted or performed. The act of creating is identical with the speaking of the words. God's words are not simply intended to be part of the prologue of Genesis 1 but are also thought to have been constitutive for the created order. What God says frames the created order. His words possess a logical priority to creation. And in this fashion God's speech acts tell us both that he is a communicative being and one whose communication is logically prior to our existence as communicative beings. Humankind speaks because God speaks. Words matter to humans because they matter to God.

The silence of humankind in Genesis 1 precludes any possibility that human and divine words stand on par with each other. But clearly the divine speaking of Genesis 1 serves as a prologue for human speaking in the rest of the canon. The speech acts of God in Genesis precede but do not preclude human speech acts. In this manner the reflection of the God who speaks so powerfully in Genesis 1 must be associated with the subsequent ability of humankind to speak.

The echoes of God's speaking in Genesis 1 are heard in the divine–human conversation in the second table. YHWH-Elohim's words in the second table still appear markedly different in force and authority than do the man's and the woman's words. God commands with words. The human couple respond to those commands. God's actions towards the rest of the created order are not framed with words in the second table as are the interactions between God and the human couple. Whatever else words signify in the second table, they uniquely connect God with humankind.

In the liturgy of creation in Genesis 1 the reflection of Elohim in humankind is unmistakably connected to the relational character of humankind. The immediate context of Genesis 1:26–27 mentions male and female after the initial designation of the *imago Dei*.[17] Karl Barth's well-known insistence that the 'male' or 'female' of Genesis 1:27 defines the *ṣelem 'ĕlōhîm* of Genesis 1:26 seems initially plausible.[18] It is warranted at least in the aspect that the *ṣelem 'ĕlōhîm* of Genesis 1:26 must be congruent with creatures whose existence is

---

[17] Grenz's (2001) discussion of the Barthian contention that the *imago Dei* is constituted by the male or female claim is most helpful. He both affirms the importance of the male or female claim and also places it in the larger construct of the 'community' themes present in the canon.

[18] Barth (1958: 195) wrote, 'Could anything be more obvious than to conclude from this clear indication that the image and likeness of the being created by God signifies existence in confrontation, in the juxtaposition and conjunction of man and woman which is that of male and female?'

wrapped up with the relationship between male and female. Barth abstracts too much from the concreteness of the gendered language of Genesis 1:27, supposing that the male or female construct conceptually stands for a face-to-face encounter between people.[19] This is true, but the text cannot be neutered and it must be remembered that 'male and female' point at a relationship of difference. Genesis 1 sets the stage for the marriage relationship elaborated in Genesis 2:20–25. While the use of the male or female does not appear to be grounded in any sort of sexual or gendered resemblance to God, it does call attention to a covenantal relationship of difference and similarity.[20] This is how both Mark's and Matthew's Gospel interpret the use of 'male and female' in Genesis 1:27. In Mark 10:3–9 and Matthew 19:1–7 the writers connect the creation of 'male and female' of Genesis 1 with the covenant of marriage established in Genesis 2. By all accounts they are not incidentally connecting the dots, but rather move without comment from Genesis 1:27 to Genesis 2:21 as if no explanation were needed, as if the connection were natural and necessary.

The consequence is important. In the liturgy of creation the reflection of God shines against the backdrop of an integral human relationship – male and female. That relationship in turn is a sign pointing to God's identity as personal and relational. In the immediate context of Genesis 1:27 the language of male and female underwrites the affirmation that God created more than one. God created 'them'. In this, he created a plurality that was nonetheless united.

There can be little contextual doubt that the creation of male and female is the necessary prelude to the creation mandate of Genesis 1:28 to be fruitful and multiply. This mandate follows immediately upon the densely structured verse 27:

[19] So argues Hughes (1989: 18–20). Hughes supposes that Barth has read 1:27 as constitutive of the image, rather than its being an additional comment on the humans God has created. What Barth takes as the obvious existential import of the conjunction of 1:26 and 27 Hughes sees as merely two conjoined but different statements. Hughes sees the male or female construct as more nearly connected to the mandate to 'Be fruitful and multiply' of Gen. 1:28. The Hebrew construction of Gen. 1:27 argues against this, however. The primary location of male or female is as that which describes the *bārā'* (create) activity of God, rather than the consequent reproductive activities of humankind. So also does the parallelism of v. 27 suppose that male or female is intimately connected to the *ṣelem 'ĕlōhîm* rather than being merely an extraneous additional comment about humankind.

[20] See Hugenberger 1994 for a biblical-theological argument grounding marriage as constituted by its covenantal framework. Though Hugenberger's specific concern is Malachi, his argument is much wider in scope and draws attention to the echoes across the Old Testament canon.

God created man in his own image,
in the image of God he created him;
male and female he created them.

It would be a mistake, however, to argue that 'male and female' is simply a place marker for how the creation mandate to 'be fruitful' is going to be effected. Sexual difference at this point in the liturgy of creation is not a method distinct from the rest of the animal kingdom. They all reproduce 'according to their kind'. This would also be true of humankind. In part the link between days five and six over which God commands the hosts (of sea and sky on day five, and of land on day six) to 'fill the earth' suggests no fundamentally different method of procreation, namely sexual relations. Rather the emphasis in verse 27 draws attention to a different theme of the *imago Dei* – the theme of unity and plurality.

The climactic threefold use of the verb 'to create' (*bārā'*) in 1:27 appears in semi-poetic fashion. It is the third time the verb is used in the first chapter of Genesis and, as if for special emphasis, the verb is repeated three times in this verse. Following Cassuto's suggestion, this appears to be the strongest evidence that the author intentionally clumped the themes of the three phrases together in such a fashion that they would be viewed as belonging naturally in concert with one another.[21] Contextually male and female belong to this threefold emphasis and are not merely incidental to the other themes of the verse. Often noticed, but not often enough appreciated, is the interwoven character of the singular and plural in 1:26 and 1:27. God acts both in the singular and in the plural. He creates a human in the singular and he creates humans in the plural. In an account where numerical nuances are replete this must be intentional. There is no wider philosophical account of singularity and plurality (unity and diversity, individual and community) in the immediate context, but, by contrast, neither is there any doubt that the author intended the reader (singer) to notice this careful weaving together of singularity and plurality.

A multitude of interpretative explanations have been put forward in reference to the divine plural in 1:26 ('Let us make').[22] The range of alternatives include an address to creation, an address to the heavenly court, a plural of deliberation, a plural of majesty, an unfiltered

---

[21] Cassuto 1967: 48.
[22] Jónsson (1988) offers a helpful summary of the alternatives.

remnant of pagan polytheism (most doubtful), a plural of divine persons. It is genuinely difficult to discern which interpretative options are plausible given the paucity of contextual clues. Early Jewish midrash seemed to favour the angels but overall early Jewish tradition was eclectic on the question.[23] Early Christian commentary overwhelmingly favoured a foreshadowing of the Trinity in the plural of 1:26.[24] Mainstream exegetes in the first half of the twentieth century seemed assured that the Trinity could not be a part of verse 26 since the author or editor could not possibly have had any knowledge of the Trinity. The latter part of the twentieth century has paid closer attention to the grammatical and semantic issues of context, but it is safe to say this has led away from any consensus rather than towards a new post-critical alternative.

While remaining tentative, several contextual clues may nonetheless be important, especially if Genesis is viewed as a canonical unit. The verb 'to make' ('āśâ) used in 1:26 is used previously in 1:7, 1:16 and 1:25, but in each of the former cases the verb is in the first person singular. The change, then, from singular to plural in 1:26 may rightly be said to mark out this act of creating in 1:26 as different. In every other instance where this verb is used in the first chapter, even where God appears as telling something else to do something, it is used in the singular. In 1:26 the plural is used and the reader expects a partner to be named, but no partner appears explicitly. Is the partner missing or merely implicit?[25] An obvious possibility is the Spirit of God, already mentioned in verse 2 and who also appears later in Genesis (Gen. 6:3 and 41:8).[26]

It ought to be noticed further that 1:27, as introducing the result of the plural verb of 1:26, concludes specifically with a reference to a

[23] See Cassuto 1961–4, Levenson 1988 and Samuelson 1992.

[24] See Louth 2001 and Harrison 2002: 347–364.

[25] Though some commentators have suggested the plural of v. 26 need not suppose a partner, the overwhelming majority of commentators (both Jewish and Christian) have seen an implicit partner as required by the context. The two most favoured by interpreters are the angelic court and some partner within God himself. A novel suggestion by Norbert Samuelson (1992) is that God's partner is the earth, since the context of day six is the production of life on the earth, and the second table affirms that God's breath is conjoined with the dust (earth) to make human life. The close linguistic connection between 'humankind' ('ādām) and 'earth' ('ădāmâ) also suggests some role being given to the earth in the creation of humankind. However, the close connection between the earth and humankind, which clearly ought to be affirmed in context, does not lead to the conclusion that the earth is a divine partner, for nowhere else is there a reference to the earth as a divine partner in creation in Genesis, nor is there any indication that the earth stands in a personal relationship to Elohim.

[26] This is defended by Clines (1998: 447–497).

plurality of people – male and female.[27] The interplay of singular and plural appears again in Genesis 3:22 at the end of the second table, and again the mention of a plurality of humans (Adam and Eve) is close at hand. The other contextual clues in Genesis that argue for a plurality of people are the theophanies of divine plurality in Genesis 11:7; 18:1–2; and 32:28.

The strongest argument against taking the plural of 1:26 as a plurality of people is the strong polemical bent against pagan polytheism in the primeval history of Genesis 1 – 11.[28] Any plurality of persons of divine nature would have implied polytheism in the ANE context. Whatever else the author of Genesis believed, he did not believe in polytheism. And so the strongly monotheist underpinnings of Genesis may appear to mitigate against any potential misreading of the text as affirming a plurality of persons in God. But taking monotheism as the chief evidence against a divine plurality supposes that monotheism demands an account of plurality that in turn demands polytheism. Why suppose that kind of philosophical sophistication? Why suppose in fact that any clarity is demanded of plurality this early in the canon – beyond the conviction explicit in Genesis, namely that there is only one God and that he has created all there is, including an image that reflects some kind of divine plurality?

To summarize where this has led so far – the language of *ṣelem* *'ĕlōhîm* (image of God) must neither be extended beyond its contextual limits nor must those contextual boundaries be ignored in discerning the meaning of the construct. The immediate context at least signals a reflection of the Creator in human creatures. And that reflection must be considered relational in part. The context also suggests that the relation is reflected in the manner in which the creatures act in the created order. The two most visible dimensions of this reflection in the immediate context of the first table concern the dominion of humankind over the rest of the created order, and secondly the filling of the created order by humankind. The first leads naturally to the ANE background of 'image' language, and the second foreshadows significant themes the canon will take up later.

---

[27] Barth (1958) hangs the whole argument for a duality in God on the reference of 'male and female' in v. 27. The problem for Barth is that the duality in God does not appear to be a sexual duality as implied by 'male and female'. However, the duality Barth infers from 'male and female' may well be the prior construct of which 'male and female' is but one kind of expression.

[28] See Hasel 1974 and Hamilton 1990.

The first table background: kings and representatives

Since the 1970s a consensus has emerged that the most important and likely background in the ANE to the use of 'image' language in Genesis 1 is that of ancient notions of royal dominion.[29] It was a common practice for ancient rulers to place statues in conquered lands representing their rule. The statue would bear some resemblance to the king, signifying his real though not physical presence in the conquered land. By so doing the king asserted his sovereignty over regions where he could not be physically present.[30]

In turn ancient kings were often described as vice-regents of distant deities, imaging those deities in the discharge of their duties. The king was a sort of living statue of the gods, representing their sovereign control on earth. Among the Mesopotamians and Canaanites royal figures were considered 'sons' adopted by the patron gods of the nation or city state to function as vice-regents and intermediaries between deity and nation.[31] In an abundance of texts the king is referred to as the 'image of god', especially so in ancient Egypt.[32] The king might have been thought to be divine or merely to rule on behalf of the deities. In either case the royal authority was rooted in the perception that the king visibly represented an invisible deity.

A further significant aspect of this ancient notion of royal dominion concerned its religious overtones. The gods who placed an image of themselves on earth in the person of the king would in turn have expected the king to place a statue of himself in the temples.

---

[29] Westermann (1984) cites 'royal representation' as the majority view in explicating the language of the image in Gen. 1. This is not an argument that thereby confines the image language in Gen. 1 to dominion, but by virtue of the presence of dominion motifs in the liturgy of creation it is imperative to keep this connection in view when explicating the theological significance of the *ṣelem 'ĕlōhîm* in Gen. 1. The lack of any mention of royal authority in Gen. 9:6 when the language of *ṣelem 'ĕlōhîm* is repeated suggests that royal dominion is not essential to it. Von Rad (1972: 57) remarks, 'This commission to rule is not considered as belonging to the definition of God's image; but it is its consequence, i.e. that for which man is capable because of it.' Bray (1991: 195–225) also correctly argues that the concept of dominion is an important dimension of *ṣelem* but does not constitute its essence.

[30] Brueggemann 1982: 39.

[31] Mathews 1996: 169.

[32] Wilderberger, as cited by Levenson (1988: 114). Mathews (1996: 169) cites an Egyptian text, *The Instruction for King Merikare* (2200 BC), as saying of Re's creation of human beings, 'He made the breath of life for their nostrils. They who have issued from his body are his images.'

Though the gods resided in heaven or on a mountain top, their real presence was communicated into the temple by virtue of the king's statue placed there. In the ancient world, where there was little distinction between political and religious authority, the language of 'image' would have carried an interwoven religious and political overtone.[33] As the image of the deity, the king exercised absolute authority over the realm, and the temple in which the king's image resided was the concrete symbol of the deity's reign through the king.

The verbs used in 1:26 and 1:28 (*rādâ* and *kābaš*) connoting this rule or dominion are very strong. They are imperial in background.[34] They signified an absolute rule, and often carried morally deficient overtones of trampling or subjugation. However, it would be wrong to suppose that the author of Genesis 1 had in view a negative moral power possessed by humankind in this regard. The immediate context tied these verbs to the task of the image as it reflected and/or resembled God. His rule was neither destructive nor morally defective, but was absolute. So it would be wise to interpret the language of rule or subdue (*rādâ* and *kābaš*) in 1:26 and 1:28 as powerful but also as morally constrained. Human rule would not be absolute, as God's rule alone was absolute, nor would it be tyrannical, for it would always be answerable to God.[35]

The ANE background would, then, argue that the peculiar purpose for the creation of the *imago Dei* was 'theophanic' – to represent or mediate the sovereign presence of God within the central nave of the cosmic temple.[36] And, in contrast to the pagan mythologies of royal dominion, Genesis 1 affirms the royal reflection in all of humankind and not simply the king or other officeholder. It is humankind considered as a whole that represents the invisible bodiless God. The entire human race is God's royal stand in.[37] Monarchs in the ANE were sometimes expected to show special concern for the poor and

---

[33] Levenson (1988: 105–110) argues that the recreation of the temple city in postexilic Israel was in part conceived as a re-enthronement of YHWH after a long period in which his palace lay in ruins, and his faithful subjects seemed abandoned and helpless. The rebuilding of the temple was a cosmic act by God to refashion his image, Israel, in the world.

[34] Ibid. 112.

[35] Brueggemann (1982: 32) probably overstates these limitations on human rule, but wisely emphasizes the connection to God's character in expounding the nature of human rule in Gen. 1: 'The image of God in the human person is a mandate of power *and responsibility*' (emphasis mine).

[36] McBride 2000: 16.

[37] Levenson 1988: 116.

destitute, but according to Genesis 1 the image bearers of God include the poor and destitute as well as the monarch.[38]

The preceding, however, is not an argument that thereby confines the language of 'image' in Genesis 1 to royal dominion, but rather to suggest that it was one important dimension of the construct. By virtue of the presence of dominion motifs in the liturgy of creation it is imperative to keep this connection in view when explicating the theological significance of the *ṣelem 'ĕlōhîm* in Genesis 1. Likewise it is important not to reduce the *imago Dei* merely to kingly authority over creation. The lack of any mention of royal authority in Genesis 5:1, when the author is clearly calling to mind the liturgy of creation and the claim that humankind is made in the likeness of God, suggests that royal dominion is not essential to the construct of the *ṣelem 'ĕlōhîm*.[39] The concept of dominion was an important dimension of the *ṣelem* but did not constitute its whole essence.[40]

After the first table: sonship and sacredness

The 'image' (*ṣelem*) language that appeared so important in the first table, occurring three times emphatically in the creation act of humankind (1:26–27), reoccurs but two more times in the Pentateuch – at Genesis 5:1 and 9:6. At Genesis 5:1 the reference is to Seth being born in the 'likeness' (*dĕmût*) and 'image' (*ṣelem*) of his father, Adam.[41] The larger theology of sonship and inheritance rights is probably in view here as Seth is distinguished from his older brother, Cain, who has forfeited inheritance rights by virtue of the crime of murdering

[38] It would also be the case that according to Gen. 1 the whole human person represents God's royal rule, without any intended emphasis on the spiritual or physical aspects of human identity carrying on this role.

[39] There is no mention of royal dominion in Gen. 9 either. Maxwell (1972: 290–304) cites Gen. 9 as a primary reason to reject royal dominion as essential to the *ṣelem 'ĕlōhîm* construct. However, implicit references to kingly authority are present in Gen. 9:2 when humankind is told that 'The fear of you and the dread of you shall be upon every beast of the earth and upon every bird of the air, upon everything that creeps on the ground and all the fish of the sea; into your hand they are delivered.'

[40] Von Rad (1972: 57) remarks, 'This commission to rule is not considered as belonging to the definition of God's image; but it is its consequence, i.e. that for which man is capable because of it.' Maxwell (1972) suggests that constructs of royal dominion in the ANE would have come far too close to idolatry to be used interchangeably with the Israelites. Bray (1991: 195–225) also correctly argues that royal dominion is an important dimension of *ṣelem* but does not constitute its essence.

[41] The fact that the word order is reversed in Gen. 5:1 from Gen. 1:26 ('likeness', then 'image') is the primary exegetical argument for the interchangeability of these two terms.

his other brother, Abel. It is not merely the hereditary connection between father and son that 'image' denotes, but more narrowly the unique legal bond that existed between the father and the firstborn. The connection of 'sonship' and 'image' here also points to a relationship of honour and respect intrinsic to the ancient familial context.[42] The son was the image of the father by virtue of honouring his father, and therefore the son came to resemble his father. What the son loved and honoured, the son became like.[43]

The connection between parent and child is also implicitly present in Genesis 1, both in the mention of male and female in 1:27 as well as in the mandate given to humankind to 'be fruitful and multiply and fill the earth' in 1:28. The contrast with the reproduction of the other animals in creation is striking. Built into the very structures of the created order is a divinely established and unique bond between human child and human parent.[44] It is analogous to but not identical with that unique bond of God to humankind. The overlapping of the constructs permits the canonical writers to borrow from one to apply it to the other. The intersection of these two constructs (image and sonship) in Genesis 5 suggests the overlap and also sheds light on the investigation into the *imago Dei*.

At Genesis 9:6 the use of *ṣelem 'ĕlōhîm* is related to the divine prohibition of murder on the grounds that God had made humankind in his image. The protection accorded humanity here is grounded in the divine regard for his own reflection. This protection is also granted as an integral part of the covenant with Noah that mirrors the covenantal administration of the first three chapters of Genesis. After the flood there is a repetition of the mandates given to humankind in Genesis 1 to be fruitful and multiply, preceded by the divine blessing. Human life is important by virtue of the fact that it has been created by God 'in his image', and now is accorded divine protection as well. The intentional taking of human life was a breaking of the divine moral fabric

---

[42] In this regard it is significant that in the genealogy at the beginning of the Gospel of Luke, Adam is called the 'son of God', as Seth is called the 'son of Adam' (Luke 3:38). This genealogy is unique among ancient genealogies for its inclusion of God in the list.

[43] Again it is important to keep in mind the democratizing tendencies inherent in Gen. 1. It is not merely males who bear the image of God, but humankind as male and female (v. 27) were and are the image of God.

[44] The echoes of this special bond are present at critical junctures throughout Genesis. The promise to Eve of judgment upon the serpent contains the promise of a future child. The promise to Noah has consequences for all his descendants. The promise to Abraham is a promise of a son, but also a promise of future generations. Certain sins are visited even to the third and fourth generations.

of the cosmos and just retribution would follow. This stands, again, in stark contrast to the manner in which animals were treated in Genesis 9. The taking of animal life was not considered a morally defective act, especially noticeable in Genesis 9:3 because animals were now given to humankind as food, a significant difference from Genesis 1.

The flood narrative, which contains the final use of *ṣelem 'ĕlōhîm* in the Pentateuch, is the last major section of narrative material prior to the emergence of the covenant with Abram/Abraham in Genesis 12 – 17. From that point forward the protection accorded human life is the presence of God rather than his reflection in humankind. For the remainder of Israel's history it was YHWH's promise to be 'with his people' that served as their strongest protection against outside threats. And accordingly the greatest threat against Israel's well-being was the removing of the divine presence from their midst. In Genesis 1 the cosmos is the temple of divine presence, but from Abraham forward the divine presence is redemptively localized and entirely outside anyone's control. The divine presence is both universal (Gen. 1) and local (Gen. 12). The relation between those two realities takes the rest of the canon to explicate.

It is with the advent of the covenant with Abraham that the language of 'image' virtually drops out of use in the Old Testament canon. The particularity of the divine beneficence falls uniquely upon Israel from this point forward, and its most tangible evidence is the theophanic presence accompanying Israel out of Egypt, in their journey in the desert wilderness and in the settlement of the Promised Land. The divine presence is not incidentally related to Israel's well-being but rather is essential to it. To Israel, the divine presence is the source of hope and the source of comfort – if not also the source of fear. God is not to be approached heedlessly nor without due honour being accorded.

The divine presence had boundaries set by God. As God determined the 'order' of creation, so he also determined the 'order' of Israel's relationship to the divine presence.[45] The two commands given to

[45] In the second table of creation (Gen. 2:4 – 3:24) when sin is introduced, God's presence becomes a threat to Adam and Eve and the serpent. The 'cool of the day' of standard translations of Gen. 3:8 might better be rendered 'in the wind of the storm' (Niehaus 1995: 155–159). God's presence in the face of unholiness is rarely ever a calm event. The threatening character of the divine presence is further emphasized in the judgments that befall Adam and Eve in the narrative, the climactic judgment being their removal from the presence of God. They are cast out of the garden. The flaming swords guarding the garden are the reminders that they will not return to God's presence except through judgment. Cain is further punished for his sin, by for ever losing a home, always to be a pilgrim on a journey, removed from the divine presence though not the divine protection.

humankind in the liturgy of creation, to be fruitful and multiply and to be stewards of the cosmic temple, were also ironically appropriate to the divine presence. The divine presence or glory filled the sacred space on top of Sinai (Exod. 19), then the tabernacle (Exod. 40) and climactically the Holy of Holies in the temple (2 Chr. 7; 1 Kgs 8).[46] Each of these sacred spaces in turn was guarded against unholy intrusion. God now guarded the sacred spaces as well as filling them.

Where, then, was the ṣelem 'ĕlōhîm? It is reasonable to argue that the emphasis upon the divine presence replaced an earlier emphasis upon the divine image. The ṣelem 'ĕlōhîm was a construct within the liturgy of creation intended to fit into a framework provided by the larger construct of the divine presence. The ṣelem 'ĕlōhîm as well as the divine presence filled and governed. And clearly Israel became the locus of the divine presence rather than the cosmic temple with the ṣelem 'ĕlōhîm at its centre, as in Genesis 1. This transfer or subsuming of emphasis depends upon seeing the role of the ṣelem 'ĕlōhîm in Genesis 1 not as an abstract principle of anthropology (e.g. about human nature, human spirituality or morality) but rather as a theological principle about reflecting and relating to God. And we should remember that the Old Testament had little interest in articulating an autonomous or universal notion of humanness, but instead was intent on situating humankind in covenant relationship to God. Humanness in the Old Testament canon is always about how humans relate to YHWH, the one and only true and living God.[47] The ṣelem 'ĕlōhîm prefigured this fundamental theological principle and there can be little doubt that the larger canonical construct of the divine presence assumed the role of providing for and protecting humankind most prominently.

The liturgy of creation in the first table suggested that the 'image' of 1:26 and 1:27 reflected the activity of its Creator in governing and filling, in protecting and proclaiming the divine presence.[48] The image was not to be equated with this activity but as derivative from its central identifying mark – reflecting God. It is important to note that

[46] With Israel's exile the crisis loomed large as to how the divine presence should be approached seeing that the temple was no longer standing.

[47] Brueggemann (1997: 451) brings this point out forcefully.

[48] The garden of Gen. 2:4 – 3:24 has strong analogies to Israel's later temple, where the presence of God is manifested at the centre of the temple structure even as the tree of life stands in the middle of the garden. See I. Hart 1995: 332. Likewise the protections accorded the divine presence in the temple bear strong resemblance to the protections around the garden as the means to keep the original couple from the tree of life in the middle of the garden.

the language of 'governing' or 'ruling' implied not only a moral character to human actions, but also an illuminating reflection of the divine activity. On day four (Gen. 1:14–19) the sun and moon were said to 'govern' the day and the night (day one). The temporal spaces were illuminated by the sun and moon, even as the sun and moon also demarcated the 'holy' days when Israel were called to worship God uniquely. When applied to the 'image' in Genesis 1:26, the language of 'governing' or 'ruling' argues for the protection of the divine reflection throughout the created order. Humankind were to reflect God's character in their actions, and therein lay their safety and security. To extend this point of 'reflection', the language of 'filling' was used first of the 'animal kingdom' on day five but secondly and more centrally with respect to the image bearers in 1:28. 'To be fruitful and multiply' carried the connotation of increasing or expanding the illumination of the divine reflection throughout the created order.

Prelude to idolatry

If indeed *ṣelem 'ĕlōhîm* was subsumed within the larger construct of the divine presence, notice should be made of *ṣelem* later in the Old Testament canon. Outside Israel's primeval history (Gen. 1 – 11) *ṣelem* did not occur again with *'ĕlōhîm*, nor with any other positive designations as a reflection or representative of God. Most often *ṣelem* was used of a physical object intended as a sign of foreign gods. In those contexts (2 Kgs 11:18; 2 Chr. 23:17; Num. 33:52; Amos 5:26; Ezek. 7:20) there are always negative overtones associated with the reflection or image. These are graven images or idols.

The danger of idols in Israel was of paramount importance and has led some to suppose that this danger led to the virtual absence of any uses of *ṣelem 'ĕlōhîm* after Genesis 9.[49] There is not any substantive warrant for the use of images in Israel because of this very danger. Some have argued that since *ṣelem* had negative connotations in every other use in the Old Testament, the writer of Genesis 1 may be communicating that humankind is merely an image, belonging to the world of perishable objects.[50] It may well be that *dĕmût* (likeness) softens the negative and wider overtones of *ṣelem* in Genesis 1:26, effectively undermining any claim that humankind was an idol. The language of *dĕmût* simply connoted that humankind was, in some

---

[49] This is Barr's contention (1968: 11–26).
[50] Samuelson 1992: 121–122.

undefined sense, like God.[51] Others have suggested that the meaning of ṣelem 'ĕlōhîm must be left intentionally vague because of the danger of idolatry and the attendant Old Testament conviction that images always tend towards idolatry.[52] It may seem strange given all the dangers, then, that the liturgy of creation uses ṣelem as the appropriate designation for humankind.

The conundrum disappears if there is a conceptual continuity between the ṣelem 'ĕlōhîm of Genesis 1 and the pervasive idolatry later in the Old Testament canon. If 'image' and 'idol' are related, there may be liturgical purpose behind the presence of the former and the absence of the latter early in the canon followed by the absence of the former and the pervasive presence of the latter later in the canon. 'Image' and 'idol' were not identical constructs, but the general contours of each overlapped in striking ways as well as fitting together under the more general conceptual umbrella of the divine presence. Both of these constructs (imaging, idolatry) are centrally liturgical in nature. Both carry connotations of 'reflection' as well as relationships of honour or worship. The danger of graven images lies in the manner in which they draw the human heart towards false gods. The dignity of the imago Dei was its ability to reflect and relate to the true and living God. Both imaging and idolatry were associated with the work of a sacred artist: in the latter case God, and in the former case humankind. And both appeared in communal settings of worship. The imago Dei was crafted in the cosmic temple of Genesis 1. The graven image was crafted by the human heart to supplement (or replace) the God whose reign was supreme over all.

As image bearers of God, humankind served as an alternative to all other images. Of all God's creatures they were uniquely able to reflect and relate to him. In their calling to 'fill' and 'govern', humankind reflected God. They also illuminated the created order by reflecting the divine presence. By contrast, graven images drew humankind in the opposite direction, reflecting the creation rather than the Creator. The graven image need not to have been merely a substitute for God, but rather to provide the occasion to reimagine his place and purpose. They turned the human heart into its own end, rather than that which was to seek God above all.

The canon began with God's creation of a self-image. The plot was greatly complicated when his self-image became a maker of

---

[51] Sawyer 1974: 418–426.
[52] Clines 1998: 475.

self-images.[53] From that point forward God mediated his presence in a different manner. Whether humankind still reflected him was beside the point. The main point of the story of redemption became the entrance of God's presence into the created order through divine representatives – in the covenant with Abraham, in the burning bush with Moses, on Sinai with Israel and in the temple with Solomon.

It is not surprising to find these themes of reflection and relationship at the other end of the canon as well. In the eschatological picture of God's consummating work these themes of reflection or illumination and relationality were again highlighted. In the new heavens and new earth there will be no need for the sun or the moon, for 'the glory of God gives it light, and its lamp is the Lamb' (Rev. 21:23). The relational theme comes out most strongly in the affirmation that 'The dwelling place of God is with man. He will dwell with them, and they will be his people, and God himself will be with them as their God' (Rev. 21:3).

The journey from Genesis 1 to Revelation 21, however, is fraught with danger, despite the promise that the divine presence will guard and guide God's people. The praise of God as Creator, begun so eloquently in Genesis 1 with the liturgy of creation, will reach its consummated end in Revelation 21. Along the way the pull towards idolatry proves almost irresistible, and it is to that part of the story that we turn in the next chapter.

---

[53] Jack Miles (1995: 21) overstates the point but nonetheless is headed in the right direction when he writes, 'the plot begins with God's desire for a self-image. It thickens when God's self-image becomes a maker of self-images and God resents it.'

Chapter Five

Turning the *imago Dei* upside down: idolatry and the prophetic stance

Idolatry is rooted in forgetfulness – forgetting what God
has done for Israel. Fidelity is rooted in remembering.
(Halbertal 1992: 35)

After creation – whence is the image?

It is often a point of theological curiosity why the language of 'image
of God' (*ṣelem 'ĕlōhîm*) occupies a place of such enormous proportions in the history of theology even though it is used with surprising
infrequency in the biblical canon. Representatively Berkhouwer
writes:

> It is indeed rather striking that the term is not used often at all,
> and that it is far less 'central' in the Bible than it has been in the
> history of Christian thought. This apparent discrepancy vanishes,
> however, when we note that Scripture's references to the image of
> God, whenever there are such, have a special urgency and import-
> ance. Furthermore, there is the possibility that Scripture often deals
> with the concept of the image of God without using those exact
> words, so that we surely should not a priori limit our investigation
> of the concept to considering only places where the term itself
> is used.[1]

The point is important though it probably ought to be qualified
further. Theology has too often not paid enough attention to the
language of the biblical text, but it is also the case that the biblical
text can use a variety of terms to represent similar realities. It may be
the case that the theology has wrongly fixated on the image of God

---

[1] Berkhouwer 1962: 67.

as the defining essence of what it means to be human, while it is also the case that the image-of-God language does provide important clues about the story of humanity told across the biblical canon. It may be that the absence of the image-of-God language after Genesis 9 is in fact an important part of the story, even if it is not a significant philosophical construct from which a general theory of human nature arises.[2]

There is a theological dynamic in which the language of the *image of God* is manifested across the breadth of the canon, though the language itself changes. The very change of terms across the canon is itself indicative of larger theological points.[3] This is clear in at least two ways: at the point where the language of image drops out, the language of idolatry becomes prominent; and secondly the re-emergence of the language of 'imaging' is most strongly connected to the arrival of Jesus Christ, who is both the restorer of the *image of God* and the one who ultimately breaks the power of the idols by overcoming the temptations of the evil one.

The shape of the canonical story suggests that the overriding dimension of the image to the original is that of worship, honour, completion and satisfaction, and conversely suggests that the sub-verting of the relationship of image to original is that of perversion, corruption, consumption and possession.[4] Conceptual overlap of the two canonical constructs of 'image' and 'idol' illuminates in turn a central Christian conviction, namely humans are made in such a way as to yearn for something beyond themselves that will grant them significance.[5] This yearning leads them in two different directions – towards a remnant of desire for their Creator and conversely towards an emerging new desire to replace their Creator with something in the created order over which they exercise control. This is not a general

[2] It is important to remember that Scripture rarely ought to be interpreted as spelling out a general philosophical theory on anything. It may provide constraints on general theories of a philosophical sort, but the very genres represented in the canon strongly suggest that the Bible is not a textbook of large philosophical theories. This point is made nicely by Wolterstorff (1984).

[3] This important claim assumes that the canon functions theologically as a covenant document and thus it is important to understand the interpretative horizons across the canon in which any context is embedded. See Horton 2002 and Lints 1993.

[4] As C. Plantinga (1995) argues, sin should be construed as a large umbrella of terms rather than only one sort of behaviour. The predominant terms suggest a defacing or destroying of that which is positive and constructive. In this sense sin is conceptually a parasite on righteousness.

[5] Berkouwer is one of the few theologians in the twentieth century who has drawn the connection between the *imago Dei* and idolatry. His treatment is insightful and influential in what follows. See Berkouwer 1962.

theory of human nature, but concerns simply and specifically a dynamic in the relationship of Creator, creature and creation.

Consider briefly the obvious overlap of the two constructs. Both contain connotations of reflection. Image language is suggestive of mirroring or reflecting, as a statue serves the function of imaging a dead war hero. In the ANE idols likewise reflected the deities to which they pointed. In fact the Hebrew term for 'image' (*ṣelem*) had the semantic range to include idols as well. At an explicit level both carried the substantive denotation of making visible that which was not readily seen. The *imago Dei* was/is the visible representation of the invisible God. Idols were the visible representations of deities, who though they did not exist, nonetheless exerted powerful influence. Both constructs in their religious usage connoted a demand for worship. The prohibition of idolatry entailed a ban on the worship of other gods. The 'image of God' was a title given to humans as creatures called to worship their Creator. Both constructs in this way defined an essential aspect of the creature–Creator relationship.

It is significant that though the language of 'image' (*ṣelem*) was largely positive in the primeval history of Israel (Gen. 1 – 11), almost every other instance of *ṣelem* outside that context is pejorative. It took on the denotation of a sign that pointed representatively at a foreign god (cf. 2 Kgs 11:18; 2 Chr. 23:17; Num. 33:52; Amos 5:26; Ezek. 7:20). It became allied with a host of other Hebrew terms casting a pejorative tone onto Israel's dalliances with these foreign gods. Other terms for idols included *pesel* (Exod. 20:4; Deut. 5:8; 7:25; 27:15; Isa. 44:10–20) (carved or graven image), *tĕrāpîm* ('family idols'; Josh. 24:14; Judg. 17:5; 18:14–20; Hos. 3:4; 1 Sam. 19:13), *'āwen* ('plain idol'; Deut. 32:21; Isa. 66:3; 41:29) and *semel* ('carved likeness'; Deut. 4:16).

The semantic similarity of the two theological constructs (image and idol) across the canon is a small clue that helps us understand better the dynamic at work in worship. The Bible often speaks of this dynamic in terms of the connection between the sacred artist and the work of art created. Humans are made by the divine artist as his reflections. The idols were made by the human artists, and in an ironic twist the human artist became a reflection of the idol. This dynamic of 'being made by' and 'being made into' underwrites both constructs (image and idol) and makes them radically different from each other.

To understand this is also to understand the manner in which the idols subverted Israel's security. YHWH was the sworn protector of Israel. As he had made them, so he would be with them. In Israel's loyalty to YHWH came their security and significance. The idols could grant no protection to Israel in the face of the threats that surrounded them. Nor could they answer Israel's pleas for help and mercy. The idols promised great blessings but could not deliver on those promises.

In the ANE kings were believed to function as vice-regents of distant deities, imaging those deities in the discharge of their duties. In Israel idols were thought of as images of these same distant deities. Surrounded by nations where idol-making and idol worship was common, Israel were called to be unique. There were to be no material images of an invisible deity among the Israelites. In neighbouring cultures carved statues abounded as the visible representations of invisible deities in whom the hopes of the nations resided. These gods often acted in arbitrary fashion and demanded fealty on the part of their human servants. The full power of the distant deities resided in the concrete idols and became an ever present reminder of the obligations that fell upon their human subjects. By contrast in Israel there were to be no carved images because God had already made a concrete image both visible and tangible to all who would look. That image was nothing less than the man and woman of Genesis 1:26.

The danger of idolatry for Israel lay in the tendency that emerged to try to find a compromise between the exclusive demands of YHWH's commands and the promises of the idols. The idols represented the false gods and thereby exerted pressure upon Israel to chase after security and significance, a security and significance the gods could never provide. It was the chasing after idols that altered the nation's identity and made the longing for security and significance precarious. The more Israel chased after the security promised by the idols, the less secure they were. Israel were already in a covenantal relationship to YHWH, redeemed from bondage in Egypt and brought to a land flowing with milk and honey. YHWH was no ordinary local deity. And Israel were called to relate to him in peculiar ways as a reflection of the peculiar God he was.

The subversion of those 'peculiar ways' was the underside of the canonical witness regarding the *imago Dei*. Idolatry was the conceptual 'turning upside down' of the originally intended relationship of image to original. Idolatry construed Israel's identity (and representatively human identity) on terms opposite those revealed in creation. The creature made a god in its image, in whose shadow the creature's identity was cast. Promising blessing, the idol created bondage. Promising protection, it created insecurity.

Divine fidelity and the image

Within the narrative of Israel's canon their identity as the people of YHWH was rooted in the original calling to image him. And this 'imaging' called them to a relationship of intimacy with their Creator or covenant Lord, which they were to reflect in all their relationships. The original mandate to image YHWH was theologically turned upside down with the idolatrous pursuit of meaning or purpose apart from him. Yet YHWH remained faithful to his people or image. His fidelity stood in contrast to his people's infidelity. This was one of the reasons why the language of idolatry emerged at the point where the language of imaging receded after Genesis 9. The focus of the covenant history from that point forward was upon YHWH's actions in redeeming or renewing Israel. The dialectic of YHWH's faithfulness and Israel's unfaithfulness animated large portions of the Old Testament narrative from Genesis 12 onwards. There were important signposts along the way of a new work of the Spirit in the hearts of Israel even when these promissory notes appeared marginal to the primary plot line. Abraham's faith, Moses' leadership, Ruth's fidelity or David's remorse all pointed at future works of the Spirit, but they quite clearly ran against the grain of the normal pattern of Israel's dispositions.

The promise of an enduring divine presence even in the midst of human unfaithfulness was a central dimension of the new kind of covenant promised to Abraham and his descendants. The exodus from Egypt was undoubtedly *the* redemptive event in Israel's history that proved God's promises of enduring presence were trustworthy. The exodus was not an event that simply resided in Israel's memory. It was an event that defined YHWH's fidelity to his people for all the generations that followed. It was the event above all others that interpreted Israel's plight across their history in the face of many dangers. As God had rescued them from slavery in Egypt, so he would rescue them from present dangers. The promise of YHWH's presence was certain in the present because of what he had done in the exodus.

But the narrative of Exodus was also followed quickly by the precarious journey into the Sinai wilderness. Israel seemed uncertain about their fate in the desert. Where they had pleaded with God for help while enslaved in Egypt, they now complained to him for the conditions they experienced in their new-found freedom outside Egypt. They did not know where food or water would come from, nor how they would navigate through the desert wilderness. Their constant grumblings prompted a surprising series of displays of YHWH's faithfulness to them. Geographical guidance was provided by a pillar of fire at night and a moving cloud during the day. Water came from a rock. Bread descended from heaven. Quail were mysteriously provided. It would have seemed reasonable to suppose that gratitude would naturally flow from Israel's experience of God's good gifts in the desert. Contrary to expectations, however, Israel could not quite accept that God would continue to provide for them. Their uncertainty was a striking and unexpected part of the story. They believed their own eyes in the face of danger, but their memories of God's concrete and tangible actions on their behalf seemed very short indeed. They knew the danger that confronted them in the harsh wilderness. They seemed less sure about the God who remained hidden from view if also abundantly compassionate in all his actions towards them.

God had promised Moses that he would bring the people out of Egypt in order to establish a covenant with them at Sinai. It would be a covenant established on the basis of his abundant kindness towards them. The exodus from Egypt was not only to escape slavery but more importantly to establish them as a people who worshipped their God and only him. He brought them out of Egypt to Mount Sinai in the middle of the wilderness for one primary purpose – to worship. At the base of the mountain they were instructed that Moses would be heading up the mountain to meet YHWH. The instructions were clear that the people were not to come up the mountain. It was Moses alone as their mediator and representative who would meet YHWH face to face. After receiving their instructions, Israel pledged fidelity to YHWH and to keep their distance from the mountain.

God granted Israel a glimpse of his glory at Sinai. The mountain was shrouded in clouds and poured forth smoke and fire. The earth surrounding it trembled. Israel were on holy ground in God's looming presence, though that presence remained hidden behind the glory cloud. Israel's instinctive response was fear in the face of the hostile environment. They believed that if they set their eyes directly on God, they would die from his overwhelming presence. Their great hope was to be near God but their great fear was to be too close to him. They realized they had to be the right distance from him. Too close and they would be shattered by his holiness. Too distant and they would lose his protection. With YHWH there was a paradox of presence. He promised to come to his people at Sinai in the sight of all the people, but also promised that no one would see him. God's presence was visually an absence. The divine theophany was still largely a mystery. Represented in geographical terms, the narrative of the exodus was clear that space and place represented theological coordinates in the covenant.

Through the mouth of Moses God recalled the historic act by which Israel had been created. Israel were told that their deliverance from Egypt had been a re-enactment of the creation story. God brought them out of the land of Egypt, out of the house of bondage and granted them life in and by his presence. They existed as a people because of God's gracious act of deliverance and the promise of his ongoing presence in their midst. These were the realities that more than any other were theologically linked to the New Testament witness of the Gospel of Jesus Christ. God came to his people and delivered them from bondage and promised to be with them to the end of the age.

The Decalogue and the diatribe against idolatry

The ceremonial granting of the law at Sinai (Exod. 20) was not an abstract legislative event. The law given was covenantal in shape and scope. It cemented kinship bonds that carried with them obligations.[6] Israel were bound to YHWH and YHWH to Israel. The preamble to the covenant ceremony at Sinai began with the words 'I am the LORD your God, who brought you out of the land of Egypt, out of the house of slavery' (Exod. 20:2). Here articulated was the history recorded that grounded the claim that YHWH was also the suzerain of the covenant. He was the one who was duly authorized by virtue of his actions to stipulate the nature of the relationship established with Israel – he was Lord.

The first law was the central principle of the covenant relationship established at Sinai. Israel were to have no other gods before YHWH. Theirs was a relationship whose bonds were not to be violated by the entry of any third party into the unique intimacy of the relationship. YHWH was to be Israel's greatest desire and greatest delight. They were to honour him above all even as he loved them uniquely among all the peoples on earth.

The underlying claim was that YHWH would have no rivals to his place in Israel's life. They were not to seek to control the relationship

---

[6] See Cross 1998: 3–21 for a detailed defence of the familial qualities to the covenants of Israel. Also see Hugenberger 1994 for an extensive development of the claim that marriage is the archetype of the covenant between YHWH and Israel.

nor supplant it with other deities they could control. YHWH was not Israel's possession who would come at their beck and call. He would in the future as he had in the past incline his ear towards Israel and show them great acts of mercy, but the divine will could not be bent by Israel's desires. Rather Israel were to delight in that which YHWH delighted in and to desire that which he desired.

YHWH understood well Israel's natural disposition to stray from the intimacy of this relationship. The desire to control their own destiny, to have gods that were more like them and who could more easily be manipulated ran deep in their hearts. There were no other gods like YHWH. It is not an abstraction to say there were no other divine beings who were maximally great. There were no other gods in the meta-physical universe. There was not a pantheon to rival YHWH. There were no other beings omnipotent, omniscient and omnipresent. Why then would YHWH enact laws about other gods if in fact, ontologically speaking, there were no other divine beings? It was because the fragility of the human heart disposed it to yearn for security on its own terms. This disposition was made all the more dangerous when it was under-written with the power to create gods in their own image and imagination. This points at the reality that idolatry was not in the first instance a cognitive error (believing in other gods) but a fallacy of the heart (yearning for control).[7]

The gods created in the deep recesses of the human longing for security were dangerous in a surprising fashion. Though they did not 'exist' in an ontological sense, they exercised enormous sway over those who had made them. They took on a virtual life of their own. This was the other side of the first commandment made manifest in the second commandment, 'You shall not make for yourself a carved image' (Exod. 20:4). The command was a recognition of the power to craft idols for the purposes of safety to replace or supplement YHWH. The language of 'image' (ṣelem) echoed back to Genesis 1 – 9, where it represented the sacred quality of the divine creation of humans. In the second commandment the language of 'image' had been turned upside down theologically and represented the profaning of humans in their divine-like activity. The warning against making carved images was a warning against mistaking the created order for the Creator. The rest of creation was not the source of significance and safety, though it often posed the most imminent threats to that safety and significance. Storms, famines, military enemies all posed

[7] Halbertal 1992: 23.

great dangers to a small nomadic group of Semitic tribes in the ancient world. In the context of the desert wilderness Israel must have heard the warnings of the second commandment with a tinge of fear. How were they to combat the forces arrayed against them if not for their own cunning and craftsmanship? But to ask this question was to see what the heart of the second commandment was centrally articulating – Israel's security had already been warrantied by YHWH.

The great danger was that Israel would be led astray by their own desires. Those desires would eventually remake Israel in their own image, wherein their identity would mirror the 'carved images' they had made to protect themselves. Israel would become like the gods they chased after: fragile, lifeless and fleeting. In essence the second command was intended to protect their identity as image bearers of the divine Creator, secure in his covenant love for them and his promise to be with them always. Israel (like the rest of us) were tempted to define the meaning of life as internal to their own desires and perceptions. Inevitably this led to a 'thinning' of self-identity wherein they became 'minimal selves',[8] wholly contingent on the gods they had made for security. YHWH's remarkable love for Israel was intended to fill their hearts with security and comfort in the face of great danger. The answers to the threats they faced lay not with acting on their ever-expanding desires but in facing up to the reality that they were divinely appointed representatives, whose security and significance were rooted in the God they imaged.

God and God's name came to represent identical realities in Israel's history. Naming throughout the ANE was more than merely attaching a verbal sound to an object or person. A name denoted the significance of the object or person. It was no surprise, then, that the third commandment 'You shall not take the name of the LORD your God in vain' (Exod. 20:7) followed straightforwardly from the second. If the second command pointed at the peculiar character of God in opposition to the deities represented by the 'carved images', then it followed that he had no ordinary name nor should be named as any ordinary object. Profaning the name of God was prohibited precisely because he was not like any thing or person in the world. He was not an ordinary piece of furniture of the universe. He was not to be thought of as part of the created order, nor to be treated as an idol made from the created order.

---

[8] This term is borrowed from Lasch 1986. Gergen (1990) makes many of the same points but speaks rather of the self, which is so filled with desires that it cannot any longer see the possibility of being 'fulfilled'.

In our modern technological culture, names do not mean much. Our children are given names because we like the sound or associate them with a pleasant memory. Names are often thin images for us that do not point at thick realities. The Lord's name was different. It had a unique denotation and therefore carried weighty connotations. Because it was unlike any other being named, God's name was sacred in this sense. His name also rested on his people. God had Solomon build a temple for his name where his redemptive presence abided (2 Chr. 6). Jesus was the name above every name (Phil. 2). Names were special in these covenantal contexts. The third commandment recognized this reality and in this sense affirmed that God's reality was not transient as was that of the idols. His name illuminated this. Israel were to protect that name and thereby were called to reflect his glory, character, mercy and righteousness.

The fourth commandment drew attention to the reality that Israel were to recognize that all of time belonged to their God. The Sabbath command reserved not simply a day for religious activities, but oriented all of time around that Sabbath practice. It was a command rooted in creation and was to be a perpetual principle of the created order. The created order was constructed in such a fashion to remind God's people that time was sacred. The sun and moon were created for signs and seasons (Gen. 1:14). In this sense the pattern of work followed by rest and satisfaction was the divine pattern imprinted on creation by the Creator from the beginning. The seventh day, which literarily never ends in Genesis 2, was the climax of the six days of labour. Human security was not grounded in human labour, but human labour was given significance in the divine order of creation. The six days pointed at the consummation of the week in the Sabbath enjoyment by Israel of their God.

The Sabbath principle was an overarching principle which affirmed that God was the *telos* of creation. The Sabbath was not an accidental or contingent part of Israel's history, nor was it fully defined by any local covenant administration. It was not subsumed under any other cultic principle. All of life belonged to God, but he did not belong to Israel. The Sabbath principle was a piece with the first three commandments that affirmed he alone was God. It was also repeated in Exodus 31 as the means to sum up the sanctity of the covenant YHWH was reaffirming with Israel at Sinai. The affirmations of the Sabbath command in Exodus 20 and 31 served as bookends for the giving of the law at Sinai, and reminded Israel that theirs was a sacred identity because of the God whom they worshipped.

The claim that God alone was God, adumbrated in the first four commands, got refracted in the succeeding six commandments, which concerned responsibility towards one's neighbour. Jesus interpreted the Decalogue with this twofold structure, and added the comment that the second (love your neighbour) is like the first (love the Lord your God) (Matt. 22:39; Mark 12:31; Luke 10:27). The second is 'like' the first precisely because the neighbour is like God. The neighbour is an image of the living God. The neighbour is not God, but is like him.

The Decalogue served to underscore the threat that idols played in Israel's life. The idols did not threaten YHWH, for the deities they represented did not exist. But they threatened Israel's well-being, because Israel were those who 'made' the idols. Promising great blessing, idols created great addictions. As God had made humankind in his image, so idols remade the very humans who had made them. The people became like their idols. This was nowhere more forcefully portrayed than in the golden calf episode of Exodus 32. Here is the paradigm episode of idolatry in the Old Testament.

The golden calf – the 'great sin' of idolatry

From the exodus event forward in Israel's history the greatest danger to the removing of the divine presence was idolatry in the midst of Israel. The landmark text in this regard is Exodus 32, which records the golden calf incident. It is a paradigmatic text whose echo across the rest of the Old Testament serves as a pungent reminder of its enduring significance for Israel's identity. It served as a template for all of Israel's unfaithfulness to YHWH – all future episodes of idol-making were interpreted in the light of the paradigm episode narrated in Exodus 32.

The theological context of idolatry in Exodus 32, as we have noted, is found in Exodus 20 and particularly in the second commandment. The prohibition against graven images sets the narrative stage for the 'great sin' of Exodus 32. Against the backdrop of Exodus 20 the violations of Exodus 32 are brought into sharp relief.

Running from Exodus 32:1 to 33:6, the account of the golden calf episode is carefully crafted in the book of Exodus. It is carried along by a descent and ascent movement and takes place on two geographical planes. At the foot of Mount Sinai the people gather at the outset and it is here that Moses confronts the idol-makers in the middle of the story. The story also ascends to the top of Mount Sinai where Moses and YHWH carry on an unusual conversation in two parts. In the first part Moses intercedes on Israel's behalf for God's mercy, appealing to the divine character as the grounds for that mercy. In the second part Moses intercedes for mercy but now without appeal to the divine character – instead he appeals to his divine appointment as Israel's intermediary. The descent of Moses from Sinai and then his ascent back up the mount serve as the central theological geography of the story.[9]

In a story too well known for our own interpretive good, the action begins in Exodus 32 with the people grumbling about Moses being gone too long up the mountain in the midst of the cloud and fire and smoke. The Israelites are in the wilderness after their departure from Egypt with the purpose at Sinai being the renewing of the covenant between YHWH and Israel. Warnings are given to Israel not to come near the mount lest they see God and perish. On their behalf Moses has ascended the mountain, as the mediator for the people, to meet with God face to face.[10] After a period of time, Israel suppose they have lost their leader and cry out to Aaron.[11] The reminder is made that Israel have a continuing sense of wandering in the wilderness and should not trust in (and fear) what they can see rather than in what they cannot see, namely in the God who created all they can see. Fear and rebellion are ambiguously mixed in the hearts of Israel. They cannot understand how God can care for them in the wilderness, most especially without their anointed leader present. They fear what they know all too well – a hunger in their belly. And so from their Egyptian experience they lean on the religious

---

[9] Hendrix (1990: 211–217) suggests that the episode has a clear chiastic structure revolving around Moses' question to the people 'Who is on the Lord's side?' in 32:26. The parallels in the narrative before and after that climactic question are very intriguing.

[10] The narrative portrayal of the encounter between Moses and the divine presence remains as the abiding validation of Mosaic authority.

[11] There is some difficulty in the translation of *'ĕlōhîm* in 32:1, when the people cry out, 'Up, make us gods [*'ĕlōhîm*] who shall go before us. As for this Moses, the man who brought us up out of the land of Egypt', and again in 32:4 after the golden calf has been made, the people proclaim, 'These are your gods [*'ĕlōhîm*], O Israel, who brought you up out of the land of Egypt!' The term *'ĕlōhîm*, which normally refers to God, has twice earlier in the book of Exodus (4:16; 7:1) referred to Moses as leader (*'ĕlōhîm*). That has led some to suppose that the sin of the golden calf is not an attempt by the people to replace YHWH but rather to replace Moses. The passage, however, does not point in this direction, since the divine displeasure is overtly about the people's rebellion against YHWH. However, it should be said that the mediatorial role of Moses foreshadowing the mediatorial of Christ does not allow for an absolute division between the leadership of YHWH and that of Moses. As the story of Miriam (Num. 12) manifests, to speak a word against Moses on some occasions was to speak a word against YHWH.

habits of those former days. They craft a molten image of a cow that will give them food in the desert.[12] The idol is probably modelled upon the agrarian idols of Egypt from whence Israel has recently come. The account strongly affirms that the ritual creation of the golden calf is performed in direct disobedience to YHWH.[13]

The narrative then shifts to the top of Mount Sinai and grants the reader a sense of divine perspective as it recalls God's abject disapproval of the making of the golden object. The passage depicts God's displeasure as hot anger. Then comes the wonderfully bizarre conversation between Moses and God. They seem to argue about who is finally responsible for leading Israel. Moses appears to scold God for forgetting his promises and pleads with him, as if Moses is a famous defence lawyer, telling God that his reputation will be destroyed in all the surrounding parts if, having brought the people of Israel out of Egypt, it is now discovered that he has brought them out only to destroy them.[14]

The reader seems well aware that YHWH is in fact responsible for Israel's redemption from Egypt and further that Moses has acted (mostly) faithfully to lead Israel out of Egypt on YHWH's behalf. However, in a surprising turn, Israel attributes responsibility for their exodus to the golden calf they have just made (Exod. 32:5). YHWH, in the cloud on top of the mount and seeing the calf, tells Moses that the Israelites are 'your people, whom you brought up out of the land of Egypt' (Exod. 32:7). Moses responds in turn by reminding God that they are 'your people, whom you have brought out of the land of Egypt' (Exod. 32:11). The question of 'belonging' is the critical question in the narrative, and continues throughout the rest of the canon. To whom do the people belong? And to whom do they confess ownership? These are the questions of identity at the heart of the story

[12] A helpful analysis of the narrative of the calf idol and its Egyptian background can be found in Childs 1974: 558–567.

[13] A generation ago there emerged a view in minority sections of historical-critical scholarship that the golden calf was made as a pedestal for Israel's God, rather than as an alien deity. This was not an uncommon practice among Egyptians (or Babylonians depending on whether the Exodus text was pre-exilic or post-exilic). On this rendering the making of the golden calf should not be seen as a rejection of YHWH, but rather as a harmless religious practice carried over by the Israelites from their days in the land of Egypt. This view came under sharp criticism from exegetes who considered the final form of the text, for the text itself portrays the divine displeasure with the golden calf as straightforward and without any hint of considering the act as harmless. For an early rejection of the pedestal interpretation see L. R. Bailey 1971: 97–115.

[14] Looking through the eyes of Moses, the text seems to suggest that he wins the case and God reluctantly changes his mind, influenced by the powerful rhetoric of Moses.

of idol-making in Exodus 32. YHWH's covenantal ownership of Israel is threatened by their attempt to grant ownership rights to the idols. And significantly, Israel's security is threatened in this change of ownership. Their purpose and significance become as fragile as the calf that can be made one day and smelted out of existence the next.

Joshua accompanies Moses down the mountain, hears loud singing and supposes first that it is the sound of preparations for war. Moses comes closer to the camp and realizes a drunken orgy is going on, focused around the golden calf in the middle of the camp. His anger burns hot, the same description of YHWH's reaction earlier in the story. And so, in a surprising reversal, Moses' descent down the mountain is followed by an enactment of swift and severe judgment upon the idol-makers, although he has previously pleaded with YHWH to eschew judgment upon Israel. This is not surprising if we realize that Moses, as the mediator of the covenant, is called to intercede on Israel's behalf when in the presence of God and to represent YHWH faithfully when in the presence of Israel. Moses is fulfilling both of these roles, though they appear in tension in the story line.

Moses has brought the stone tablets down the mountain. Representing the terms of the covenant, the stones serve as the written record of the covenant relationship between Israel and YHWH.[15] When Moses' anger burns hot, he throws the tablets onto the ground, smashing them and thereby signalling a break in the covenant relationship between Israel and YHWH. He deals with the covenant breakers by smelting their golden calf, grinding it into a powder, spreading it across the water and forcing the people to drink it. Symbolically the calf is to provide food for them, and now Moses requires the idol to make good on its promise. The people physically take the idol into themselves, and from this point forward in Israel's history acts of rebellion are characterized by appeal to the calf's attributes – a stiff neck, a hard heart, ears that cannot hear and eyes that cannot see. The sensory malfunction language often used in the Old Testament with reference to rebellion resonates from here in the golden calf episode. A dead idol is now imprinted in the living rebellions of the people.

Moses returns to the mount seeking to make atonement for the sins of the people. He stands before the presence of God and pleads with him to forgive Israel's sin. If God refuses, Moses asks that his name be blotted out of the book God has written, the book of the covenant

---

[15] Moses refers to the stone tablets as the 'tablets of the covenant' in Deut. 9:11.

that is also the book of life. God responds that those who have sinned will be blotted out his book. He calls Moses to lead the people, reminding Moses that he (YHWH) will bring judgment and remember the sins of the people. The passage ends by suggesting that God smites the people because of their 'great sin' with the golden calf. The rebellion of Israel has resulted in judgment, a judgment Moses both prevents and is powerless to halt. He is the divinely ordained mediator for the nation of Israel but is not accepted as a atonement for sin to God on behalf of Israel. The nation is preserved as a result of Moses' pleading, but covenant forgiveness does not occur through his mediatorial pleading. Moses is the leader of the people of Israel but is not their Redeemer. He is a divinely appointed mediator, but does not successfully atone for Israel's sins. Moses pleads on behalf of Israel when in the presence of God, and in their time of greatest trial does not abandon them. God goes so far as to suggest that he will make of Moses a great nation in place of Israel. At that moment Moses foreshadows the work of the Messiah who, when tempted by the people's rebellion, refused to be separated from them. Moses points ahead to this radical identification between the Messiah and the people of God, not because they are worthy but because God has appointed him.

The judgment meted out by Moses in the camp of meeting has been swift and terrible, but the final divine judgment is yet more sobering. Moses' ascent of the mount near the end of the episode is followed by the final manifestation of God's righteous anger towards the idol-makers. YHWH delivers a promise that his presence will not reside in the midst of a rebellious people with the haunting words 'I will not go up among you, lest I consume you on the way, for you are a stiff-necked people' (Exod. 33:3). God will not dwell in the midst of an idolatrous people. This represents the gravest threat to Israel's well-being. Their safety is now in doubt because God will not be with them.

Upon closer scrutiny it was not simply any act of disobedience that was the root cause for the removal of the divine presence. Rather the character of idolatry, of creating an image of an alien deity, was the conceptual undoing of the original act of being created in the image of God. Israel's collective act effected an ironic reversal of the original covenantal arrangement. Rather than illuminating the created order with the reflection of YHWH, Israel now sought their significance and security from the created order. In due course they became like the idol they had created: stiff-necked, hard hearted, with eyes that could not see and ears that could not hear. They became images of an idol.[16] Yet the idol was itself powerless to effect the hoped-for help. The idol was not simply an alternative deity, but a false god, which strictly speaking was no god at all. YHWH's insistence that no other gods be worshipped (Exod. 20:3) did not imply that there were in fact other gods, but rather that worship or honour was proper only as directed towards him. Worship fashioned the worshipper into an imprint of the object worshipped. Worship of the one true and living God brought life in all its purpose, dignity and security as a consequence. Worship of the false gods refashioned worshippers in the image of the inanimate creation. And for this reason the honouring of the golden calf was the theological turning upside down of the original order of creation.[17]

Covenantal identity and idolatry across the Old Testament

The canonical echo of the Sinai episode reinforces its significance for Israel's future relationship to YHWH. Israel's peculiar identity rested in their peculiar honouring of YHWH and keeping their distance from the gods/idols of the other nations.[18] Their place and security in the land was contingent upon this peculiar honouring. Honouring God was an expression of covenantal loyalty to the God who granted them significance and safety.

In Moses' song recorded in Deuteronomy 32 there is a strong interplay between the idols made by the people and the people themselves. The idols are 'no gods' and God shall make Israel yearn to be like the 'no people' who follow the 'no gods' (Deut. 32:21). The crafting of the idols have robbed them of their identity – their identity as living people has been undermined. The idols, which represent the 'no gods', have sucked the life out of their hearts.

The human person as an image stood as a stark alternative to the images (idols) of the nations. The images/idols of the nations were dangerous precisely in the manner in which the golden calf was dangerous. They undermined the covenantal loyalty crucial to Israel's significance and safety. In 2 Kings 11:18 the images/idols of Baal are destroyed with the recognition that they are powerless competitors to

[16] Cf. Keyes 1992.
[17] Cf. Ellul 1985: 86–96.
[18] See Brueggemann 1988 for an extended discussion of the relationship of idolatry and the public identity of Israel in the ANE.

YHWH for Israel's loyalties.[19] Israel cease to be YHWH's possession and become instead the possession of the idols. As the canon so often portrays, to be near God is to have life, but to be far away from him is to experience a living death.

In Numbers 33 YHWH issues a warning to this effect regarding the gods/idols that Israel will confront on the other side of the Jordan when they go in to possess the Promised Land. The 'rebellion in the desert' serves as a pungent reminder of Israel's fragile status. YHWH instructs them to 'destroy all their figured stones and destroy all their metal images and demolish all their high places' (v. 52) when they enter the Promised Land. The 'metal images' are the idols of the Gentile gods. They are the concrete representations of the gods in whom the Gentiles trust. The rehearsing of YHWH's great redemptive act of exodus is to be an ongoing ritual in Israel to remind them of his mighty acts on their behalf. It is often accompanied by the corresponding rehearsing of Israel's 'rebellion in the desert' – a reference to the making of the golden calf. YHWH's faithfulness is contrasted with Israel's unfaithfulness. This is not an indicator of Israel's hopelessness, but rather of the very great assurance that YHWH will fulfil his promises to them.

Moses reiterates the significance of the golden calf episode at the end of Israel's wilderness years in the context of the people renewing their vows to YHWH and promising continuing fidelity (Deut. 9). As the people prepare to enter the land of Canaan, the land promised to their fathers, Moses reminds them of their rebellion during their Sinai desert experience: 'Not because of your righteousness or the uprightness of your heart are you going in to possess their land' (Deut. 9:5). The primary evidence of their unrighteousness cited by Moses is the making of the golden calf. It serves as the paradigm of their stubbornness. He goes on to cite several more instances of their rebellion in the desert, but the episode upon which the template of rebellion is interpreted is straightforwardly the making of the golden calf.

In language hearkening back to the golden calf episode, Israel's prophets often referred to Israel's hard-heartedness, stiff necks, their having ears but not seeing and having eyes but not seeing (cf. 2 Chr. 30:8; 36:13; Neh. 9:16–17; Job 41:24; Isa. 6:9; 32:3; 44:18; Jer. 5:21; 7:26; 17:23; Ezek. 3:7; 12:2; Pss 95:8; 115:5–6; Zech. 7:11). The golden calf had sensory organs but they did not function. So Israel had the capacities to see and hear and taste YHWH, but these capacities were

---

[19] A parallel account is found in 2 Chr. 23:17.

as defective as the golden calf's sensory organs. These terms of sensory malfunction became common terms for Israel's unfaithfulness to YHWH. They were connected to taking on the imprint of the idol that was made at the foot of Mount Sinai. It is not that all rebellion was identical, but rather the wide conceptual template of idolatry was large enough to bring some notion of coherence to Israel's rebellion against YHWH.

Often the summaries found later in the canon of the large narrative of YHWH's actions in redeeming Israel recalled the two typological acts in the desert – the exodus and the golden calf. So Nehemiah's recounting of redemptive history at the rebuilding of the temple calls to mind both God's great act of deliverance from Egypt and Israel's 'great blasphemies' with the golden calf (Neh. 9:21). Stephen's speech, which reviews the history of Israel, likewise connects Moses' rule as the redeemer of Israel in bringing them out of Egypt by the power of God and the people's rebellion in requiring Aaron to make a golden calf to lead them (Acts 7).

The hymnody of Israel likewise connects the great act of God's redemption in the exodus and the contrasting act of their infidelity in the episode. Psalm 106:19–21 offers these words:

> They made a calf in Horeb
> and worshiped a metal image.
> They exchanged the glory of God
> for the image of an ox that eats grass.
> They forgot God, their Savior,
> who had done great things in Egypt . . .

The retelling of the story of Israel's redemption is contrasted with the story of their making of the idol. God brought Israel out of bondage and gave them life. In turn they made idols and became like their idols, without life.

Throughout Israel's history no single term was used for idols, but the variety of terms in their own way drew attention to the likeness of the idol to the gods, and the devastation wreaked by the idol on the idol-maker. Idolatry was a large umbrella of concepts, all of which pointed at the subversion of the original relationship between image and original. The idols were described as 'metal images', 'carved images', 'figured stone', 'idols of wood and stone, of silver and gold' (Deut. 29:17) – often drawing attention to the stuff out of which the idol was made, and thereby drawing attention to the reality that idols belonged to the class of things 'made' rather than to living people.

If the language of 'image of God' (*ṣelem 'ĕlōhîm*) drew attention to the visible representation of the living God, the language of idol drew attention to the visible representation of the gods that were not living. Jeremiah refers to the idols as scarecrows. They look like living people but are not able to talk or walk (Jer. 10:5). There is no life in the idols and therefore they cannot be life-giving. Although they look like living creatures, they neither have life in themselves nor represent living gods.

Isaiah loomed large over the Old Testament in the period of the monarchy, and it was he who offered the clearest and richest denunciation of idolatry in the period. In Isaiah's denunciation of the idols there were several important insights into the genuine theological dynamic of idolatry. Occurring during the reigns of four different monarchs, the second half of Isaiah opens with four spiralling poems, each in turn having to do with the confrontation between YHWH and the gods of the nations. By turns they are legal in tone and by other turns like proverbs in tone. At times YHWH appears to be prosecuting a case against Israel's covenant-breaking practices. At other times Isaiah appeals to the irrationality of idolatry itself and seems to be pleading for Israel to recognize the inner logic of their practices with the idols. That inner logic is the crafting of communal significance and safety with the labours of their own hands. Here is the central contradiction of idolatry. It is God who formed humankind. It is God who has designed humans for significance. And it is God who protects his creatures. Time and again Isaiah reminds Israel that the Lord has created them and has redeemed them (Isa. 40:26, 28; 41:14; 42:5; 43:1, 3, 14–15; 44:6, 21, 23–24). Idolatry is the strange turning of this reality on its head, by suggesting the very objects of one's making are the means by which one can gain significance and security.

In Isaiah 40 idol-makers are portrayed as Godlike in their creative abilities. But unlike God, idol-makers get faint and their strength wears out. They become hungry and thirsty, as all humans do. God not only does not grow weary or faint, but in that familiar refrain of Isaiah 40:31,

> they who wait for the LORD shall renew their strength;
>   they shall mount up with wings like eagles;
> they shall run and not be weary;
>   they shall walk and not faint.

At a certain point Isaiah's argument becomes almost satirical. The idol-maker cuts down trees to make his idols. He uses some of the wood for cooking, some for heating and the rest to make his idols. As if the scraps of wood are worthy objects of worship. The satire unveils the genuine mechanics of idolatry. The idol-maker ventures to make his own idol as the means to control his own significance and safety. The tragic consequences are that this activity becomes an endless chasing after an ever elusive goal.

In Isaiah 44 the idols are said to be 'empty/nothing' (*tōhû*; v. 10), hearkening back to the formlessness and void (*tōhû wābōhû*) of the earth in Genesis 1:2. The emptiness of the idol, however, belies the arrogance of the project. Idol-makers suppose they are actually creating a deity.[20] The rhetorical question therefore is, who indeed can possibly make their own god? What sense does it make to say that the god who made us is made by us? The inner logic of idolatry is exposed. The idol is nothing, but the project of idolatry is itself dangerous. There is no need to fret about idols from one vantage point. They are representatives of beings that do not exist. They are empty/nothing. But from another angle the project of idolatry is theologically dangerous, for it seeks to turn the created order upside down – the Creator becomes the created, and the created becomes the Creator.

Idolatry and adultery

The language of marital infidelity is a root metaphor in the Old Testament to make explicit the character of idolatry (cf. Exod. 34:14–15; Lev. 20:5; Judg. 2:17; 1 Chr. 5:25; Isa. 1:21; 23:17; Jer. 3:8–9; Ezek. 16:17; Hos. 4:12–13; Mic. 1:7).[21] 'To go whoring after other gods' is a common way to speak of idolatry (Exod. 34:15–16; Lev. 20:5; Ezek. 6:9; 20:30).[22] Picturing God as the bridegroom and Israel

---

[20] Though the idol is but a concrete representation of deity, Isaiah claims there is such a close identity between the sign (idol) and thing signified (god) that no real separation exists between them. The idol is fully invested with the sacred presence of the god.

[21] The exegetical trajectory linking idolatry conceptually with adultery probably begins with the original placing of *imago Dei* together with the male or female reference in Gen. 1:27.

[22] It is important to note that though idolatry is illuminated by adultery, it is not the case that the two should be seen as identical, nor should the prevalence of the marriage metaphor be mistaken for considering it more dangerous than idolatry itself. The church has often reflected more upon the danger of corrupt sexual relations than corrupted relations of idolatry. Adultery has too often assumed larger proportions in a Christian ethic than idolatry, whereas in the Scriptures it is the reverse. Cf. Geller 1997: 117–122.

as his bride allowed the history of Israel to be construed as a sacred romance. The bridegroom searched out the bride and redeemed her from troubles she had brought on herself that had been thrust upon her by outside forces. The bride was not always careful to keep interlopers out of the marriage bed. She too often played the harlot.

The big picture of the sacred romance uncovered one very important dimension, though not the only dimension, of the relationship between YHWH and Israel. Within the metaphor of marriage Israel are depicted as desiring the very things YHWH abhors, suggesting not simply that Israel have broken laws (they have) but also and more profoundly that they have let their hearts go astray. Israel are to desire the things YHWH desires and to delight in the things in which he delights. The language of sexual desire for the idols connotes that sense in which the whole person has gone astray, and though momentarily pleasurable, ultimately the alliance with false gods is destructive of the whole person and community.[23]

By way of contrast Israel's true bridegroom (YHWH) manifests a genuine love for the bride – a love both glorious and enduring. In the later prophets especially (Isaiah, Jeremiah, Ezekiel, Hosea; Isa. 61 – 62; Jer. 25; 33; Ezek. 16; Hos. 3) YHWH's faithful love of Israel stands in stark contrast to their faithlessness. The use of marital language to depict YHWH's relationship to Israel points back to the Genesis account, where the marriage relationship was an integral part of the order of creation, and most especially a reflection of the triune God. The sense of 'belonging to each other' that marriage affirmed was rooted in the original relationship of Elohim to our human parents. They were created in God's image as those who naturally belong to God, not as possessions but as people in relationship. Those created in the *imago Dei* were called or privileged to be in a relationship of intimacy with their Creator.

The story of the sacred romance between YHWH and his bride was corrupted by the parallel story of Israel's marital infidelity where she continually prostituted herself before other gods.[24] Israel's bridegroom is continually described as 'compassionate and gracious, slow to anger and abounding in love and faithfulness'. The terms of intimacy are unmistakable. YHWH loves his bride. By contrast Israel are those who 'broke faith with the God of their fathers, and whored after the gods of the peoples of the land' (1 Chr. 5:25). Israel's

---

[23] See Ortlund 1996 for an extended treatment of these themes.
[24] The linking of prostitution and idolatry is forcefully portrayed in Exod. 34 in the aftermath of the golden calf episode.

behaviour is not a result of a cold calculation as to which gods can deliver on their promises. Rather it is like a consuming lust for love. The worship of other gods by Israel reflected an insatiable need for love detached from any ties of faithfulness.

The marriage relationship is an integral part of the created order as manifested in the typological passage of Genesis 2:18–25. So the covenantal bonds between YHWH and his bride are wired into the fabric of redemptive history. Those whom God redeems enjoy a covenantal sense of belonging to him, not as mere objects of his possession but as people in an intimate relationship. YHWH is jealous of this relationship. He protects it and goes to extraordinary lengths to keep his bride pure in the relationship.

The graphic depiction of Israel's infidelity to YWHW becomes all too concrete in the tragic story of Hosea. Hosea is a faithful Israelite in a period of moral declension in the northern kingdom. Israel are mired in a period of serious idolatry and Hosea's words come 'like a bear robbed of her cubs' (Hos. 13:8). And yet in the midst of the divine indignation at Israel's spiritual adultery YHWH expresses an undying love for his bride. That radical love is given voice in the living parable of Hosea and Gomer. The faithful Israelite prophet is to marry Gomer, a prostitute of ill repute as a vivid analogy of YHWH's marriage to his unfaithful bride, Israel. In the marriage between Gomer and Hosea three offspring are produced, all of whom seemed destined for despair. They are named Jezreel, No Mercy and Not My People. One can only imagine the parental discouragement regarding their prospects. During the marriage, Gomer shows no signs of forsaking her former ways and continues the nightly trysts with a variety of lovers. At some point Gomer abandons Hosea entirely and ends up prostituting herself into slavery. Humanly speaking, Hosea's relief must have been palpable. Whatever relief he might have experienced was short lived, however. He is instructed by YHWH to search out Gomer and buy her back from slavery. Hosea is to redeem Gomer and take her again as his bride. It is almost unfathomable to understand the costliness of Hosea's calling to his unfaithful bride. It remains mysterious, but, in one of the few interpreted living parables in the Old Testament, the relationship of Hosea and Gomer is directly explained against the backdrop of YHWH's unfailing mercy to his people. In the very place 'where it was said to [Israel], "You are not my people," it shall be said to them, "Children of the living God"' (Hos. 1:10). The surety of that hope lies not with Israel's will, but with the steadfast determination of YHWH.

That divine determination does not fit neatly into our moral categories. Mercy of this sort seems contrary to our intuitions about justice, even if it is also clear that justice is not undermined. The great reversal occasioned in the practice of idolatry, of turning the theological order of Creator and creature upside down, is itself reversed again in the divine determination to show mercy and love justice. The power of the idols will be broken in the strange display of YHWH's compassion most fully articulated in Jesus Christ. To the living word, the perfect image and the exact representation we turn in the next chapter.

Chapter Six

Inverting the inversion: idols and the perfect image in the New Testament

Christ is the movement of the invisible God into visibility
in the life of a human being.

(Rowe 2005: 301)

Turning the story upside down

In the New, as in the Old, Testament, the *imago Dei* is not a place
marker for generic human nature. It has a distinctive theological role
to play. That role is most clearly the unique office as a divine representative and divine reflection. In the New Testament the *imago Dei* is
most directly connected to Christ (2 Cor. 4:4; Col. 1:15).[1] In the case
of Christ he is the 'exact representation' and that by which the invisible
God has become visible (cf. Heb. 1:5 and John 1:18 respectively).[2]
Christ is the perfect image who suffers in our place and for our redemption (Eph. 5:25–26). As a consequence, human identity is most clearly
seen in Christ, the one in whom, through whom and for whom
humankind was made (1 Cor. 8:6; Col. 1:16).

By contrast idols represent the inversion of the original theological
order of representation and reflection. The idols depict an exchange
of the glory of God for the foolishness of this world (Rom. 1:23). The
practices of idolatry assumed that the gods were beings adequately
represented by objects of gold or silver and could be shaped by their
worshippers (Acts 17:29). The idol alleged to give purpose to its
followers while being created by those same followers. This paradox

---

[1] However, James (3:9) does use the term 'likeness of God' as a reference to
humankind. It seems to function in a manner similar to Gen. 1:26 and James probably
intends the phrase as a canonical echo of Gen. 1:26.
[2] 'Image' (*eikōn*) has the semantic range to signify that which is not the shadow but
the reality: 'For since the law has but a shadow of the good things to come instead
of the true form [*eikōn*] of these realities, it can never, by the same sacrifices that are
continually offered every year, make perfect those who draw near' (Heb. 10:1).

is the crux of the theological argument against the idols that echoes across the canon. It is foolish to suppose that creatures can 'make' the Creator. Equating any part of the created order with the Creator is a category mistake of the highest order. Jews and Christians in the first century would have agreed that idols remained extremely dangerous. The peculiar claim of early Christianity was that Christ alone, as the perfect image, breaks the power of the idols.

The practice of idolatry was pervasive in the world into which early Christianity was moving and appeared to be tempting even to those who professed loyalty to Jesus Christ.[3] The iconic traditions in which humanly manufactured objects represented transcendent deities pervaded the Graeco-Roman world and were difficult for newly converted Christians to repudiate in their entirety. Since there were no sharp sacred–secular distinctions in the ancient world, the religious customs associated with the temple cults were often considered normative for all citizens of the empire. Rejecting the customs entailed dissonance with imperial rule, and inevitably put Christians in danger of not being granted civil tolerance.[4] The opposite danger was just as real as well. Showing any kind of loyalty to the idols would be viewed as unfaithfulness to Christ and thereby put one's place in the covenant at risk. The number of continuing reminders in the New Testament to flee from idols is ample evidence of the recurring temptations of idol practices for early Christians (1 Cor. 10:14; 1 John 5:21).

In what follows I outline the contexts for the New Testament discussion of human identity and idolatry. Those contexts deal with the Christian interaction with Jewish backgrounds to idolatry and also with the then present practices of idolatry in Gentile lands. The theological arguments against idolatry appear quite similar in both of these contexts, though the practices described as idolatrous would have been quite different. Theological warnings about idolatry in the New Testament led inevitably to expositions of the redemptive mission of Christ as the 'perfect image'. Surprisingly it turns out that God does have a visible image, and though this may appear as grounds for accusing Christianity of idolatry, the apostles claim that the visibility of Christ as the image of God is what inverts the corrupted order of

---

[3] The deeply aniconic traditions of Israel, which eschewed any and all concrete images of God, found a ready home within early Christianity as well. The diatribes against idolatry found in Exodus and Isaiah, for example, would have been readily accepted by early Christians. See Achtemeier 1999: 43–61.

[4] Barton (2007: 152–154) notes the numerous citations from Roman sites of the first century that regarded Jewish and Christian abstention from the temple cults as amounting to a hatred of humankind and a detestation of the Roman Empire.

idolatry. In Christ the Creator has entered creation and thereby recreated the cosmic order after his image. The apostle Paul in particular frames this mission by comparison of the first and second Adams, the man of dust and the man of heaven respectively (1 Cor. 15:48–49). We look in particular at the manner in which their respective temptation narratives illuminate the struggle of desires at the heart of idolatry. In the final part of this chapter we turn to consider the Pauline material on living as images of the perfect image.

Setting the context

The problem of idolatry crops up most frequently as a boundary question between Christians and the Gentile cultures into which Christians went as the gospel departed Jerusalem for Asia Minor. Idolatry was not a prominent theme in the disputes between Christians and Jews of the first century.[5] Both of these groups had explicitly repudiated the religious practice of temple idolatry. At a confessional or covenantal level there was no theological space in Judaism or Christianity for the idols. This is not to say, however, that the temptations towards idolatry did not run strongly in both groups. The admonitions to avoid idolatry and the condemnation of idolaters makes little sense otherwise. Though there is a strong conceptual chasm between the worship of idols and the worship of the living God, it was difficult for many converts to distinguish the two entirely.[6]

In contrast to Judaism and Christianity the Gentile nations thought of idolatry in positive terms. Idols were physical representations of the gods worshipped locally. In each location where temple worship took place the idols reflected the sacred presence of the people's peculiar deities. As the cult of the emperor grew in the first century, temples were constructed to the Graeco-Roman pantheon, with the emperor now included.[7] These 'national' gods and their idols were to be revered across the breadth of the empire. It is unclear exactly when the emperors themselves were included in the pantheon, but the cultural pressure to honour the emperor in semi-deific terms was very much present in the second half of the first century.[8] This is the point

[5] On this point see ibid. 142.

[6] Marcus 2006: 152–164.

[7] On the historical background to the imperial cult see Price 1984. For the issues surrounding Christianity's interaction with the imperial cult see Klauck 2000.

[8] For illustrative differences over the relative dating of the book of Revelation, based on difference as to the dating of the growth of the imperial cult, see Biguzzi 1998: 276–290 and Warden 1991: 203–212.

at which Christianity was spreading throughout the empire – not yet posing any military threat to the Romans, but quite clearly not in step with the religious impulses of the empire.

In Jesus' interaction with the Pharisees there is only one prominent place where idolatry is even implicitly mentioned.[9] In Mark 12:14 the Pharisees ask Jesus whether Jews should pay taxes to Caesar.[10] The question implicitly relates to whether the image of Caesar on the coins used to pay taxes constitutes idolatry. The reasoning would have been straightforward. Caesar claimed final loyalty over the citizens of the empire and therefore his image would have been construed as an idol by devout Jews. This would have led to the inevitable conflict between Caesar and YHWH, who likewise claimed final loyalty of all the citizens of his empire. The coin requested by Jesus did in fact portray the emperor as the *Pontifex Maximus* (High Priest) of the Roman religion. According to the inscription on the reverse side of the coin, Caesar was himself 'Augustus', a term connoting a quasi-deity to be worshipped.[11]

In his response to the query of the Pharisees Jesus understood the challenge of coins, but resisted the assumptions behind the questions. Treating another human as God was wrong. But the question was about what practices constituted treating another human as God. Did paying taxes to Caesar entail treating him as God? Jesus reasons that the emperor can be recognized as important to the well-being of the empire without also attributing to him divine powers. In this sense Jesus is demythologizing the emerging emperor cult – Caesar is not God – while also granting the emperor his right to collect taxes for the well-being of the people.[12] This became the pattern for Paul in dealing with food offered to idols. If the idols were treated as divine, then Christians should abstain from the food offered to them. But if the idols were treated simply as blocks of gold or silver, then eating food offered to them was permissible.

The emperor cult seemed to have become more aggressive after

---

[9] There is some conjecture whether the issue of idolatry is raised at the trial of Jesus as recorded in Mark 14. There are witnesses at the trial who accuse Jesus of saying that he will destroy the temple made with hands. The expression 'made with hands' (v. 58) might well have evoked the biblical expression for an idol, since that was a central difference between an idol and the true and living God. Cf. Barton 2007.

[10] The parallel accounts can be found in Matt. 22:15–22 and Luke 20:19–26.

[11] The background to this issue of tribute paid to Caesar can be found in Hengel 1989: 100–105. Hengel notes there were riots in AD 26 when Pontius Pilate introduced the coins into Jerusalem with Caesar's image on them.

[12] Marcus 2006: 157.

Jesus' death, extremely so under Domitian (emperor AD 81–96), who demanded a test of loyalty from all Roman citizens because of his claim to deity. This would have been quite different under Augustus and Tiberius, the emperors in Jesus' time, where there appeared to have been no such test.[13] Relinquishing the coin to the tax collectors by Jesus amounted to no more than an affirmation that Caesar possessed some form of civil authority. Undoubtedly had Jesus been confronted with a claim about the alleged deity of the emperor, he would steadfastly have denied it. Towards the end of the first century, Christians faced this precise situation. As the book of Revelation manifests, martyrdom was the cost of refusing the emperor's test of loyalty and denying his claim to deity.

Idolatry and the Gentile mission

When we turn to the rest of the New Testament, the central discussions of idolatry occur in the context of the mission to the Gentiles. The reason is apparent – engagement with the Gentile world meant confrontation with the pervasive and persistent temple cults of the Graeco-Roman world that openly flaunted their loyalty to idols.[14]

The Gentile mission was already a source of considerable friction for other reasons among the earliest Christians. At the Jerusalem Council in Acts 15 the apostles effectively headed off a schism in the early church by affirming together that Gentile converts to Christianity need not be circumcised. According to the council this would no longer be a boundary marker between Jewish and Gentile Christians. However, the apostles were clear that the Gentile converts ought to avoid idolatry – most likely a reference to the temple cults of Gentiles, where idol worship took place in honour of local as well as imperial deities. These temple cults were often accompanied by temple prostitutes, whose presence underscored for the apostles the connections between idolatry and adultery.[15] The linkage between the two was important because the New Testament continued to insist that the bond between God and his people was a marital bond rooted in

[13] Ibid. 163.

[14] Barton (2007: 143) comments on the regularity of New Testament depictions of idolatry in Gentile contexts, 'The reason is not hard to find. The ever increasing range and intensity of engagement with Gentiles – traditionally understood within Judaism as . . . idolatrous – necessarily demanded attention to the rules of purity, since these rules constituted the principal means of guarding against disqualification from participating in God's holiness as God's chosen ones.'

[15] Rosner 1991: 21–30.

covenant fidelity. The sexual licence taken by unfaithful marriage partners was a concrete reflection of the infidelity expressed by God's covenant partner.[16]

The animal sacrifices of the temple cults were also prohibited for Christians. More ambiguous was the question of whether Christians could eat the meat that had previously been slaughtered in the temple sacrifices. Knowing where and when idolatry stopped and started was not easy. Was it permissible to buy meat from the idol sacrifices that found its way into the marketplace? Was it permissible to eat in Gentile homes where it was probably idol meat that was being served? How close or how distant should a Christian stay from the culture of idolatry that pervaded most Graeco-Roman towns?

At the Jerusalem council the apostles drew a strong line around the temple cults themselves, and thereby drew a strong linkage between idolatry, sexual immorality and certain kinds of food. The apostolic decree at the conclusion of the Jerusalem council was representative of these concerns. That decree insisted that Gentile Christians, as would have been the case for Jewish Christians, should 'abstain from the things polluted by idols, and from sexual immorality, and from what has been strangled' (Acts 15:20).[17] They were to resist the dominant religious practices of the Graeco-Roman world in which they lived while being fully cognizant of the need to survive in that idolatrous world.[18] Practical questions therefore remained about what constituted resistance to the Gentile religious culture and what counted as accommodation to these practices. The changing shape of Gentile culture meant that the early church would have to continue to wrestle with these questions far beyond its initial contexts.[19]

Sex and food rules were interpreted in the light of idolatry because of their probable connection to practices surrounding the temple cults of the first century. It is somewhat surprising then to find that greed is included as an idolatry-related vice. Greed was not related to the temple cults of the Graeco-Roman world; yet Paul denounced

[16] The language of 'covenant' is more often circumscribed in Scripture to include Israel in the Old Testament or the church in the New Testament. However, it should not be forgotten that covenant descriptions are also used with respect to God's relationship to all humankind and to all of creation. This would suggest that breaking covenant with God is not only something that Israel and/or the church commit, but also of which humankind in general are prone. See Horton 2006.

[17] Similar connections between idolatry, sexual immorality and certain kinds of food can be found in Rom. 2:2; 1 Cor. 5, 8; and Gal. 5.

[18] Marcus 2006: 152.

[19] On this question of the practice of resistance and accommodation by the early Christians to idolatry see Bonnington 2007: 107–119.

greed as idolatrous in Colossians 3:5 and Ephesians 5:5. No other vices in the New Testament are listed with such a straightforward connection to the larger theological umbrella of idolatry. Why greed? The initial clue may come from the reminder that idolatry is fundamentally defective worship. It is rooted in the desire to replace God as the proper object of worship. There are any number of alternatives that the Scriptures confront, including money. Jesus' warnings against trying to serve two masters, God and Mammon, is a pungent reminder that money is all too often treated as an alternative deity to the living God (Matt. 6:24; Luke 16:14). Treating greed as a form of idolatry is simply an affirmation that money, though not intrinsically evil, can nonetheless be worshipped as an idol.[20]

Theologies of idols: Romans 1 and 1 Corinthians 10

Repeating the pattern of argument from the Old Testament, the New Testament uses two primary arguments against idolatry. In the first case idolatry is prohibited on the grounds that it inverts the relationship between Creator and creature. Creatures cannot suppose that their Creator can be shaped according to their own imagination. It was God who made humankind and all efforts to fashion a god in their own image is thereby to be resisted. A second ground for the rejection of idolatry is that idols represent gods that do not exist. If this is so, then the idols are merely objects of gold, silver or stone.[21]

Throughout the New Testament the apostles affirm the inverted relationship between image and original. There is most especially for Paul a fundamental flaw of logic in the practice of idolatry. The transposing of the original and the image is a fatal contradiction. Paul lays out the argument at greatest length in Romans 1, and applies it most directly in Acts 17 in his confrontation at Athens with the Gentiles.

In the context of the epistle as a whole, Paul's argument about the idols/images in Romans 1:23 can be isolated for our purposes, though

[20] See Rosner 2009 for a thoughtful and nuanced treatment of greed in the New Testament.

[21] Achtemeier (1999: 46) refers to three New Testament arguments against idolatry: 'first, the inadequacy of material objects to serve as divinities or their representations; second, the inadequacy of any figuration to serve as a representation of the Creator of all reality; and third, the impossibility of tolerating any other deity than the one God, of whom no representation can be made'. I've combined Achtemeier's first two arguments into one. Whereas his third argument calls to mind the spiritual adultery arguments of Hosea, I've highlighted the echoes of Isaiah's argument in 1 Cor. 10 – the idols represent gods that do not exist. These arguments obviously do not conflict with each other.

its significance for the Jew–Gentile tensions throughout the letter are important. A great and terrible exchange takes place in the practice of idolatry according to Paul's account. The glory of God is exchanged for images of every sort of creature: men and birds and land animals and even reptiles.[22] The Creator is exchanged for creatures from the heavens, the earth and the seas.[23] This description of the tragic exchange of idolatry is a Pauline way of providing a big picture of human corruption. Never intended as an exhaustive account of human corruptions, nonetheless idolatry is a large conceptual framework by which Paul describes the moral transformation of humans.[24] Created good, they became sinners through their own folly. They exchanged the truth for a lie. It was an inherently irrational exchange, and this is exactly why the reversing of the exchange is not primarily an intellectual matter. Redeeming what was corrupted centred on matters of the heart.

In Romans 1 the apostle issues the familiar canonical claim that there is no comparison between the Creator and the creature, and yet humans have persuaded themselves into thinking that other created things will satisfy their deepest longings. The apparent wisdom in this is the illusion that created things can be more easily controlled than the Creator. It is folly to suppose that created things can adequately replace the Creator without significant loss.

The futility (Rom. 1:21) in their thinking is the failure to recognize the change in their own security, all the while supposing they have determined the source of their security.[25] Yearning for greater security, their identity has become more precarious and thin. Their grasp for

[22] Rowe (2005: 289–312) argues that Paul's reference to all these classes of objects is intentional. Hooker (1960) argues that the only referent of 'image' in Rom. 1:23 is 'man', and Paul mentions the other objects only incidentally. The reason is that the apostle is building up to an Adam–Christ argument in Romans and therefore only 'man' is in view in Rom. 1:23. I think Paul has Genesis in view in the background of Rom. 1, though contrary to Hooker, I take Paul's interest in Rom. 1:23 to be more generic and less specific to the later Adam–Christ typology of Rom. 5.

[23] In the background may be a reference to the entirety of the cosmos, since birds, animals and reptiles are used as representatives of all three parts of the Genesis cosmology: heavens, earth and seas. Rather than being an account of the natural order, the threefold schema represents the totality of the cosmos. See Kline 2006 for an elaboration of the cosmic order of Genesis.

[24] Although it may have ontological consequences, the assertion of human fallenness is primarily a moral disorder. This means also that idolatry is a moral defect rather than merely an alternative cultural account of worship. Likewise the language of 'image' carries strong moral overtones. On the moral character of the *imago Dei* see Horton 2006: 101.

[25] The Old Testament background to Paul's charge of futility points in many cases at idolatry. See in this respect especially Ps. 94 and Jer. 2.

control has in fact resulted in a loss of control. They are given over to the very idols in which their hopes lie. Paul is insistent that idols will not deliver on their promises. Instead they create consuming passions in which there is no deliverance. This inverted state is surprising from one angle – how foolish humans are to suppose they can have a god on their own terms. And yet the inversion produces an entirely predictable consequence – abandoning God results in an identity crisis wherein one's safety and significance become endlessly fragile.

There are important contrasts throughout Paul's argument in Romans 1 illuminating the emotional power of idolatry. Hoping to hold down the truth, humans are held down by unrighteousness (1:18). That which can plainly be seen is exchanged for darkness (1:20–21). Though they knew God, they now do not know him (1:21). Claiming to be wise, they become fools (1:22). The glory of God is exchanged for but a dim image. The shadow is embraced rather than the reality (1:23). Refusing to honour God, they dishonour themselves (1:24). Truth is exchanged for a lie (1:25). In each of these there is a turning upside down or an inside out of the created order. This is Paul's way of 'explaining' sin. There are lists of vices in other Pauline texts that catalogue human corruptions in systematic order. In Romans 1 the intention is rather to describe the irrationality of sin and the danger of its consequences.[26] Idolatry makes no sense when considered from the vantage point of the Creator–creature relationship. Idolatry is the height of human folly. And yet in its very irrationality, idolatry has a powerful hold upon the human heart. The seat of human desire is now settled in darkness (1:21). The addictive passions now rule the heart and the stench of corruption fouls the soul. Foolishness is now called wisdom.[27]

In 1 Corinthians 10 Paul follows another familiar argument against idolatry. There he turns his attention to the Isaiah 44 argument that idols are neither living nor represent gods that exist.[28] The non-living idols represent non-existent gods.[29] Paul admonishes the Corinthians to flee from idolatry because the gods represented

[26] Karl Barth (1958) refers to the irrationality of Adam and Eve's choice to eat of the fruit for the very reasons Paul alludes to in Rom. 1.

[27] Paul reverses this contrast in 1 Cor. 1, where redemption is referred to as foolishness in the eyes of the world.

[28] There are echoes of this same argument in Rev. 9:20, where the idols are described as those that cannot see, hear or walk. In other words they are lifeless.

[29] Cf. also Acts 19:26, where Paul rehearses this same familiar argument from the prophets against idolatry.

do not exist. In this light they cannot provide any grounds for hope in the face of adversity.

Paul's concern in 1 Corinthians 10 is food offered to idols. If idols represent gods that do not exist, is there any harm in eating the meat left over from the animal sacrifices of the idol temples, which will later be sold in the market? The question is framed against the backdrop of the typologically significant episode of the Israelites and the golden calf (1 Cor. 10:7–8). Though the immediate controversy has to do with Gentile practices of idolatry, the theological grounds come from Israel's own history of idolatry.

Israel were birthed as a nation in the exodus event. It was the departure from Egypt that for ever stamped Israel's identity with the covenant-making YHWH. Paul writes of Israel's having been baptized into Moses in both the cloud and the sea (1 Cor. 10:2). They were given a new identity in these nation-defining episodes. The sea quite clearly pointed at the surprising crossing of the Red Sea at the command of Moses. The cloud pointed at the divine presence that hovered over Israel as they wandered in the Sinai wilderness after the Red Sea crossing. Paul also references the episode of the manna in Exodus 16 and the water from the rock in Exodus 17. Five times in 1 Corinthians 10:1–4 he uses the language of 'all' to emphasize that everyone in Israel has been marked by these realities.

Israel's rebellion evidenced in the golden calf episode was all the more striking when set in the context of YHWH's provisions for them. Israel had witnessed the shrines to the Egyptian gods while in captivity in that land. Though they sustained a separate identity from the Egyptians, the Israelites inevitably accommodated the surrounding religious practices to their own context. And they brought those compromised practices with them into the Sinai desert.

Paul references Israel's idolatry as a paradigm of the temptations of idolatries in Corinth (1 Cor. 10:11). The Graeco-Roman temples in Corinth were undoubtedly different from what Israel had experienced during their long sojourn in Egypt, but the pattern of idolatry was the same. Temptations arose when the Creator was confused with the creation. The idols were fashioned from wood and stone and were thereby no match for the living God. The dead idols may have been near at hand and could be manipulated for self-serving purposes, but were powerless to deliver the significance and security their worshippers so craved. They promised blessings on terms more easily manageable than YHWH's terms. The problem was that the idols never delivered on their promises. They could not, since they were 'nothing'. Their attraction was that they could easily be manipulated. Their great defect was that they were impotent to do anything. Their great danger was that they produced loyal subjects who would not question their impotence. What did this have to say to the question of eating meat offered to idols? Paul's initial response is to treat the idols with the respect they deserve, namely none. Therefore he encourages the Corinthians not to have any qualm of conscience about eating meat that might have been offered to idols (v. 25). Christians are free to share in meals in private homes that involve serving meat that has been bought in the meat market, which may or may not have been slaughtered in honour of some idol (v. 27). If God is the Creator of all, then nothing should be considered evil in itself – even meat intended for idolatrous purposes.[30] After all, meat was meat and the idols themselves were 'nothing'. However, practices associated with idol worship are prohibited by Paul. There is to be no dalliance with any object, real or imagined, that challenges God's sole unique status as the singular Creator and Redeemer. There are to be no other gods in the hearts of God's people.[31] From this angle one should abstain from eating meat offered to idols if it encourages, even in the slightest way, the practices of idolatry.

The situation in Corinth as well as throughout Asia Minor was complicated by sociopolitical realities. Unlike Jews in the Second Temple period, Christians did not have civil protections for their strange religious habits or convictions. They were accused of maligning the local deities by which cities retained their status in the empire. Jews might be forgiven for their aniconic traditions because of their own long and peculiar history. Christians, however, were a new sect and could not be trusted to refrain from revolutionary actions against the civil order and against the pantheon that legitimated that civil order. The result was that Christians often found themselves having to tread warily with their former cultural customs. They feared retribution if they criticized idol worship of the local shrines too clearly, and yet also realized that their new-found faith could not be syncretized with any polytheistic paganism of the ancient world. All of this provided the emotional tension so frequently felt in the New Testament's behavioural admonitions to Christians living in Gentile lands. They were not to cause more offence than necessary, but their commitment

[30] Achtemeier 1999: 56.
[31] Halbertal (1998: 166) cites Gamaliel in a similar spirit: 'what is treated as a god is forbidden, but what is not treated as a god is permitted'.

to Jesus also meant that all other pretenders to the divine throne must be rejected. To be in the world but not of it was a precarious vocation in the first century, even as it remains so in the twenty-first century.

Narratives of idolatry: Acts 7 and 17

Luke records two significant episodes in the book of Acts that narrate the precariousness of refusing to bow before idols. The first is Stephen's speech before the Jewish ruling authorities in Acts 7, and the second is Paul's presentation of the gospel at Athens in Acts 17. The former deals with idolatry in Israel's past, whereas the latter deals with idolatry in the Gentile present. In both cases idolatry refers to a set of practices in concrete settings rather than a theological abstraction about the metaphysics of divine existence. In Acts 7 the acts of idolatry mentioned are those of the golden calf episode of Exodus 32. In Acts 17 the idols referred to are those Paul confronts in the city of Athens. Stephen and Paul refer to these practices in the context of larger arguments about the nature of belief and unbelief. In the context of the Israelites Stephen illustrates the pattern of their unfaithfulness to the covenant with YHWH, whereas Paul illustrates the Gentile confusions about God.

In the immediate context of Acts 7 Luke notes that Stephen has been appointed to deaconal service in the young church at Jerusalem. He has got into serious trouble with the Sanhedrin both for his testimony about Jesus and his performance of 'wonders and signs' (Acts 6:8). Accused of criticizing the temple and the law, Stephen is formally charged with religious treason.[32] His defence is to tell the story of Israel in a manner to which his accusers will assent. He also tells the story in such a fashion that it highlights the pattern of idolatry of which he is accusing the Sanhedrin.[33] He does not formally deny the charges against him but rather places them in the wider story of Abraham, Moses and David. From that perspective he draws attention to the long-standing pattern of Israel's ruling authorities rejecting YHWH's prophets and entrusting their security to alliances with the nations instead.[34] That pattern now repeats itself in the Sanhedrin's rejection of Jesus.

[32] James Sweeney (2002: 185–210) argues rightly that Stephen's speech is a defence of Jesus as the fulfilment of the temple rather than a criticism of the temple as such. Sweeney's treatment is the best biblical-theological treatment of this passage in the contemporary literature.
[33] Cf. Wright 2008: 108–109 for a helpful summary of the precedents for Stephen's defence of himself by recasting the history of Israel in a new light.
[34] Dahl 1966: 139–158.

Stephen's telling of the story begins with the claim that the God of glory initiated the covenant promises with Abraham, though great hardship and trial later came to the descendants of Abraham as well.[35] In the face of hardship within Egypt Israel grew in number but also in their accommodation to the ways of the Egyptians. God's anointed prophet Moses was rejected by Israel at first. Later God graciously redeemed Israel from enslavement to the Egyptian Pharaoh by miraculously bringing them out of the land of Egypt into the Sinai wilderness. Despite this remarkable act of deliverance, Israel responded by fashioning the golden calf in the desert and placing their hopes in the idol they had created with their own hands.[36]

Stephen then appeals to the inner contradiction in this primal sin of idolatry – creatures fashioned an idol with their own hands, only then to suppose that the idol was the god who had made and given them security. Even the temple is prone to this pattern of idolatry according to Stephen. The temple was constructed by human hands under divine appointment, but could never thereby fully contain the most high God of the universe. He was not at Israel's beck and call merely because they were the ones who had constructed the house of the Lord. The works of their hands did not grant them prerogatives over the living God or his messengers. As sacred as the temple was, it too was susceptible to the corruptions of the logic of idolatry. This was nothing intrinsic to the temple as such, but rather to the attempt to control the divine presence the temple represented.[37] This is the logic of Stephen's contention that God cannot be contained in a building made with hands.[38] Neither God nor his people can be controlled by any creature's efforts.

Stephen reminds the Jewish ruling court that this narrative of

[35] Cf. Ps. 29 for background on the title 'God of glory'.

[36] Bruce (1988: 143) draws attention to the significance of 'made with hands' in Stephen's speech. In particular he notes the importance of the phrase in the Psalms where 'the idols of the nations are described as silver and gold, the work of men's hands' (Acts 6:41).

[37] Witherington (1998: 262–266) argues correctly that Stephen's defence is not an instance of anti-temple polemic. I concur with Witherington but on different grounds. He cautions against any anti-temple polemic in Luke-Acts since the temple plays a relatively positive role throughout the corpus, and further the language of 'made with human hands' need not be interpreted in unduly negative tones.

[38] Evans and Sanders (1993: 198) note the connection between the idolatry of the golden calf and the control of the temple by the Sanhedrin: 'Nothing is wrong with the temple nor with building it, but it is wrong to believe that it (and perhaps it alone) is the habitation of God. Moreover, allegiance to a temple built with human hands could place Israel in danger of repeating its earlier wilderness sin, for the gold calf had also been made by "their hands".'

idolatry is embedded in Israel's habits. The paradigm act of idolatry of Exodus 32 was followed by the continual habit of borrowing the patterns of worship from the surrounding nations.[39] Stephen cites Amos 5 as evidence from Israel's own history of the pattern of idolatry. He infers from the golden calf episode that all future idolatry, which the prophets later condemned, had its origins in the wilderness. Even the worship of Moloch and Rephan by the northern kingdom of Israel, which Amos cites, was linked to the pattern that began in the Sinai wilderness.[40] As with their fathers, they too had become like the idol in the desert – stiff necked and uncircumcised in heart. Placing their significance and security in the works of their hands resulted in their identity reflecting these very works.[41] Instead of controlling their gods, they were controlled by them.

It is not hard to understand why the religious authorities were furious with Stephen and demanded his death. Stephen had criticized the very power structures by which the Sanhedrin maintained its control over the religious affairs of Israel.[42] Those 'power structures' had been interpreted by Stephen through the lens of idolatry. The Sanhedrin's only hope according to Stephen was finally in the Redeemer sent by YHWH to free them from enslavement to themselves and the corruption of their own hearts.

The language of enslavement cut in two different ways. The Sanhedrin understood slavery in political terms and thereby refused to acknowledge that they were an enslaved people (cf. John 8:31–38). Though the Romans exercised military rule over them, they had maintained some semblance of religious freedom relative to the temple in Jerusalem. Stephen (and Jesus) by contrast uses the language of

---

[39] Phillips (2003: 159) reaches beyond Exod. 32 and connects the rebellion of the Sanhedrin in Acts 7 to Cain's rebellion in Gen. 4. Broadly speaking, both do represent paradigms of sin against kinsmen. There are undoubtedly theological patterns of rebellion that the two accounts share in common. It may well be that the closer parallel for Acts 7 in the early chapters of Genesis is Adam's eating of the fruit as the fulfilment of the promise that when he eats of it, he will be as God.

[40] Bruce 1988: 145.

[41] Pelikan (2005: 105) draws attention to the similarity between Acts 7 and 17 in the characterization of idolatry as being 'made with human hands'. Idolatry is a pattern of false worship inside as well as outside God's covenant community.

[42] It is a common theme in critical scholarship on Acts 7 to see Hellenistic bias against Judaism or a Samaritan bias against Jerusalem in Stephen's speech. Donaldson (1981: 27–52) shows why it is highly unlikely that any Hellenistic or Samaritan bias is at work in Luke's account. The problem is not Judaism or Jerusalem as such in Stephen's speech. Rather it is the rebelliousness of the ruling authorities that is the focus of Luke's account. On the alleged Samaritan background to Stephen's speech see also Mare (1971: 1–21).

enslavement to address the theological character of their own hearts. Accordingly Stephen criticizes the rulers as being enslaved to their own corruptions. Whether Roman occupation of the holy land was a divine judgment was beside the point. The problem was not political but theological. The real issue lay with the long established pattern of refusing to worship God on his terms, and thereby to find security in the works of their own hands.[43] Idolatry served as the conduit through which this long-established pattern became manifest. The practices of idolatry came under the most severe indictment, not because they were worse than all other sins but because idolatry was a typology for all other sins.

Turning now from the narrative of idolatry within Israel's history to Luke's primary account of idolatry among the Gentiles in Acts 17, the core theological moves were quite similar. Worshipping false gods or worshipping the true God falsely arose from the same mechanism – creatures inverting their rightful place relative to their Creator. The focus on the mission to the Gentiles in the second half of the book of Acts lacks the citations of Old Testament texts about idolatry as is the case in Acts 7. Common to both passages is the claim that Jesus is the rightful recipient of worship for both Jews and Gentiles. And idolatry is the theological means to explain the refusal by Jews and Gentiles to worship him.

In Acts 17 Paul confronts the common religious idolatry of the Graeco-Roman world at Athens. Saul the Pharisee was converted on the road from Jerusalem to Damascus (Acts 9). Transformed from one who once persecuted the church to one who now defends the gospel, the apostle Paul assumes a prominent place in the second half of Luke's account of the diaspora of Christians after Pentecost. Luke's narrative rendering of Paul's encounter with Gentile idolatry in Acts 17 illuminates the wider theological concerns of the New Testament critique of idolatry, while placing it in the concrete world of first-century Athens.[44]

---

[43] Witherington (1998: 274) concurs: 'In short the real issue is who is in control and gets to define the terms, nature and location of God's presence – God or the people, in particular the temple hierarchy?'

[44] Helpful historical background to the city of Athens the apostle Paul would have experienced in the first century can be found in Bruce 1988: 328–334. He writes (333) of Paul's speech, 'Probably no ten verses in Acts have formed the text for such an abundance of commentary as has gathered around Paul's Areopagus speech.' Countless sermons have also drawn attention to the similarity of contexts between Athens and present-day Western culture. Representatively see Davis 2003: 64–68 and Dunham 2006: 202–206.

Athens was a city filled with idols, which were probably more pervasive than in other cities of comparable size in the Graeco-Roman world. Its long and distinguished history had in part been tied to the heritage of temples and statues dedicated to a variety of emperors and gods.[45] The two most famous were the statues of Athena and Hermes. There were also several altars to unknown gods to ensure that no gods were omitted from their rightful place within the pantheon. The idolatry Paul confronted at Athens was a point of considerable civic pride. Unlike the charges of idolatry Stephen levelled at the Sanhedrin, the Athenian idols were considered a sign of its cultural significance. Paul's critique of idolatry in Athens would probably have struck the Athenian elites as odd.

The apostle's argument against idolatry focuses on the altars to the unknown gods.[46] These altars provided the context for engaging the larger argument about idolatry. Paul evinces evidence from the Greek poets that there must be a God who created the world (Acts 17:28).[47] The question is what the nature of this Creator God is.[48] The critical hinge in Paul's argument turns on whether it makes sense to suppose that the Creator of the world can be fashioned out of gold or silver. God created humankind; not the reverse. He is not an image that can be formed from the imagination or creativity of human artists. Paul appeals to the inner logic of idolatry rather than denouncing the practice of idolatry.[49] He claims that it is illogical to suppose that humans can find their safety and significance by creating the God who gave them meaning in the first place.[50]

[45] Cf. Zanker 1998 and Moxnes 1995: 107–132.

[46] There is some dispute as to whether there were such altars in Athens to 'unknown gods'. Witherington (1998: 521–523) summarizes the issues well, and persuasively argues that these altars would have been present in first-century Athens.

[47] The poets cited are Epimenides and Aratus. Both were probably referring to Zeus as the supreme being of Greek philosophy. Bruce (1988: 339) rightly notes that Paul's citation of these lines does not equate Zeus with YHWH, but points at some recognition in the philosophical tradition of the true nature of God.

[48] The religious tradition at Athens often supposed that the Creator god was a bare cause of the world, and little attention was given to his possible personal character. The gods of the Greek pantheon were very personal and thereby deeply flawed in peculiar ways. Paul's claim that the Creator God was both the cause of the world and personal would have been a strange idea to the Athenians. Cf. R. Bailey 1990: 481–485.

[49] C. K. Barrett (1974: 69–77) rightly notes that Paul's argument shares some sympathies with the Epicureans and Stoics in their attack on the overt superstitions of popular religion focused around the temple cults.

[50] Witherington (1998: 530) notes that Paul's argument in v. 28 assumes a common belief with the Epicureans that there is some form of kinship between God and humans. However, Paul inverts this common belief by claiming that because humans come from God, he is the one who must give purpose and meaning to them.

The close connection between idols and gods in the ancient world carried the assumption that the gods were materially present in the idols that represented them. Constructing idols supposed that the gods were not only adequately represented by the works of human hands, but that these works constrained the presence and power of the gods. Here was the dilemma to which Paul pointed. How could a god create all that is, and yet also be effectively controlled by the world that god had created?

In the context of the Graeco-Roman world the religious habits of the temple-cult system were well entrenched. Paul's challenge to the whole system would have seemed to most rather preposterous. What made the challenge to the system at Athens significant, however, was the philosophical world into which Paul was speaking.[51] Against the backdrop of the Epicureans and Stoics Luke reminds the reader that Paul is confronting the illogical nature of idolatry.[52] Paul's citations in this passage come from revered Greek philosophical poets, another reminder of the audience to whom he is speaking.[53] It is the peculiar theological commitments of the Athenian traditions that are exposed by Paul and to which he addresses himself. It is less the political patronage at the heart of the temple cult system of Athens that concern him. Rather the inner contradictions of the world view represented by the idols focus his comments.

Lest there be any doubt that Paul is pointing at an incidental difference, he closes the speech by addressing the life-and-death character of the issues involved. Divine judgment awaits all humans. The Creator God must also be the God who holds final justice in his hands. From the implicit recognition that God created the world, it follows that this God will bring the world to its proper consummation. It may have appeared to some that Paul appeared to build intellectual bridges between the Athenian's conception of God and his own. But Luke is quick to remind the reader that Paul just as abruptly tears down the bridge by referring to the resurrection of Jesus as the definitive statement about God. Though the audience apparently mocks Paul for his belief in the resurrection, Luke provides no indication that Paul is surprised by the reaction. There is an inner

---

[51] Pelikan 2005: 191.

[52] Cf. Cloy 1997: 21–39 for a helpful reconstruction of philosophical beliefs that form the context towards which Paul's speech is aimed.

[53] Wilson (1973: 207–209) points to the citation from Aratus in Acts 17:28 as evidence that Paul is concerned with the fundamental assumptions behind the logic of idolatry rather than the popular practice of idolatry.

logic to idolatry, but there is also a deep addiction to the domestication of God by the human heart.[54] Those addictions can be broken only by the power of the Holy Spirit.

The perfect image

What marks out the New Testament as different from the Old is the claim that the *imago Dei* attains a unique status in the person of Jesus Christ, not merely as a human but as the perfect image of God. This is not an abstract metaphysical claim, but primarily a confession about salvation. The claim that Jesus is the 'image of the invisible God' (Col. 1:15) is the means to establish that God is renewing, restoring or redeeming his people into his image. As the image of God, Jesus came to 'reconcile to himself all things, whether on earth or in heaven, making peace by the blood of his cross' (Col. 1:20). Christ not only makes known the divine intention to reconcile his people, but effects the work of reconciliation in his own death. In Christ those who were far off are now brought near by his blood (Eph. 2:13).

In Christ God became visible. The knowledge of God was no longer hidden. In John 1 the Word who was with and was God becomes flesh and lives among humankind in such a way that God's glory can be seen. And in John 14, in response to Philip's request to show the disciples the Father, Jesus says, 'Whoever has seen me has seen the Father' (v. 9). Knowing or seeing the Father is centrally knowing God's redeeming act in Christ. It is the soteriological function of Christ that is the focus of the New Testament. Jesus reveals God as the God who saves his people. Revelation and redemption go hand in hand across the canon.[55]

Central to any discussion of the New Testament appropriation of the *imago Dei* construct are the Pauline texts 2 Corinthians 4:4 and Colossians 1:15. In the former the apostle argues for the character of the gospel as formerly veiled but now revealed in the person of Jesus, who is the image or likeness (*eikōn*) of God. The gospel is the glory of Christ, whose light illuminates those with eyes formerly blinded

[54] Willimon (2010: 144) poignantly writes in reflection on this passage, 'Idolatry is not necessarily the pastime of the ignorant and the simple. Intellectuals play the game quite well. The God whom Paul proclaims is not just another option for human devotion, not an accommodating God content to be one among many. The God who sent the Christ is still the Holy One of Israel, a jealous deity without rivals, an exclusive lover who tolerates no competition – money, sex, philosophical ideals, institutions – who fiercely judges all idols made by hands or minds of men.'
[55] Gaffin 1987.

by idolatry. The 'god of this world' (*theos tou aiōnos*), like the golden calf did, blinds all those who seek security and purpose at its feet. The blind and dumb idol refashions its worshippers after its own image, whereas Christ, in a virtual act of recreation, restores the 'inner self' (*esō hēmōn*; 2 Cor. 4:16) in an ironic reversal the second creation being enacted by one who is also the very image or likeness of God.

In the larger context of 2 Corinthians 3 and 4 Paul draws his readers' attention to the encounter at Sinai when Moses' face shone because he had been in the presence of God. The glory of God had been reflected in Moses' face, hearkening back to the claim in Genesis 1 that humans are the images or reflections of God. Not only does Paul make the claim that Jesus is the image or likeness of God, but those who now know Jesus shine with a glory greater than Moses ever had. The divine presence has reached a redemptive climax in Christ and the glory of God shines in a qualitatively greater way than previously. The *imago Dei* is being filled with a 'greater' reflection of divine glory than that reflected from Moses.

Paul complements this description of the perfect image in Colossians 1:15 by again affirming that Jesus is the image of God (*eikōn tou theou*) and that the fullness of God dwells in Jesus. Jesus carries the full weight of divine glory. Paul also asserts that Jesus created all things both visible and invisible. Paul (like John) places Jesus in the opening act of creation as a means to argue that Jesus was the purpose, or *telos*, of creation – as God was the *telos* of humankind. 'In him [Jesus] all things hold together' (Col. 1:17), even as Paul affirms in Acts 17:28, 'In him [God] we live and move and have our being.' As the image of God, Jesus reflects him and mysteriously fills all things with that reflection. He is the new Creator, echoing his role as the original Creator.[56] As Paul argues in Romans 8:28–30, the destiny of those 'in Christ' is to be conformed to the image of the Son by the redemptive power of the Spirit. Christ is the new Creator as well as the *telos* of the new creation, even as the Spirit is the one who constructs the new temple presence of God through Christ by means of setting up Christ's (and the Father's) residence in the believers' hearts.

The *imago Dei* finds its fullest theological significance in Jesus, in whom the ironic reversal of the original reversal of sin has begun and

---

[56] In similar fashion the apostle John in Rev. 1 represents Jesus as the Alpha and Omega who is also the visible representation of the invisible God. The author of Hebrews (ch. 1) portrays Jesus as the exact representation (*charaktēr*) of God and the one in whom the beginning and end hold together.

will be consummated.[57] Jesus took on our humanity and restored its glory as the reflection of God.[58] Jesus was the royal son, on the basis of whom other sons and daughters would be adopted into the family of God. If idolatry was the theological act of honouring the creature above the Creator, Jesus was the one who reversed that theological move by reconstituting the *imago Dei* with the full reflection of the divine glory in his own person. Jesus was the true image in contrast to the false idol.[59]

While Paul rejects any image fashioned from creation to represent God, he resolutely refers to Jesus as the image of God. In Jesus' concreteness the invisibility of God is made visible. The Creator has imaged himself in the creation, all the while warning against humans taking any part of creation as the final image of the Creator. When the Creator stepped into creation, a new creation was effected. Though great mystery still attends the presence of God, the divine intention to recreate humans in the image of Christ became manifest in the life, death and resurrection of Jesus.[60] By a sovereign divine act the incarnation inaugurated the new cosmic order. The blueprint for the new cosmic order was to be found in the very one who brought that order into being. In Christ's suffering he redeemed those whom God called his own. In Christ's resurrection he defeated their final enemy, death itself.

The concreteness of Jesus made these divine plans evident. Those who are incorporated into Christ take on this divine image as well, not becoming messianic in their nature, but following the pattern of life, death and resurrection now experienced vicariously in Christ (Rom. 6).

The sharp contrast between the living image (Jesus) and the dead idols cannot be missed in Paul's argument. In 1 Corinthians 15 the apostle asserts that Jesus is the 'life-giving' spirit, who defeats our final

[57] Grenz's (2001: 223–266) reminder that the image has a significant eschatological component to it, though not explored here, is exactly right and here begs for a fuller treatment.

[58] Kline (1980:61) writes, 'In redemptive history the reproduction of the image of God in the new mankind takes place through the mediatorial agency of Jesus Christ, in whom the divine Glory became incarnate. He is the paradigm of the Glory image and he is the mediator of the Spirit in the process of replicating the divine likeness.'

[59] The language of idolatry is used in 1 Cor. 12 and 2 Cor. 6 as a way to describe the former state of those who have now come to confess Jesus as Lord.

[60] Horton (2005: 108) rightly notes that this act of recreation is historical and eschatological rather than ontological or metaphysical. It effects a reconciliation between estranged parties by means of fulfilling the just requirements of the covenant. It does not effect a substantive change in the human attributes of Jesus, nor in his divine communicable attributes.

enemy, death itself. The idols do not bring life, but instead further embed death in our nature. The theological contrast between Adam and Christ in 1 Corinthians 15 captures this same sentiment. All of humanity bears the image of Adam, the man of dust. In Adam humans inherit death as their just sentence. In the resurrection Christ's people will bear his image, the man of heaven, and will inherit an imperishable existence. Yet strangely, on this side of paradise God's people bear both the image of Adam and the image of Christ. These images are not mutually exclusive. This argues that 'image' functions not as an ontological description of one's essence, but as a theological depiction of the divided worship of the human heart. It is the question of one's theological identity, of where one finds significance and security. The idols represent the attempt to find significance and security by the works of one's own hands.[61] By contrast Jesus is the one whose significance and security from beginning to end are found not in the labours of his own hands, but in sacrificing his life for others. Though he is equal with God, he does not consider that status as grounds to assert control on his own terms (Phil. 2:6–8). Rather he willingly obeys his Father even at the cost of his own life. He is the inverted idol of God, the one who humbles himself to the point of death on a cross.

The various uses of *eikōn* in the Pauline materials form a basic conceptual unity in this regard. Christ as the image of God makes the invisible God visible. The Christologically shaped community called 'the church' bears the image of Christ in that it makes the pattern of his life, death and resurrection manifest. The false images (idols) reflect the reality that there are false attempts to make the invisible God visible, and manifest the possibility of distorting the pattern of the perfect image of God (Jesus).

In the context of the canon the (true) divine image makes God known and enacts the divine intention of redemption. According to Scripture, the community of those who image the perfect image make Christ known and proclaim the divine intention of redemption. The theological inversion of these tasks is to be found in idolatry. Through human foolishness the knowledge of God was distorted and divine redemption turned into self-justification or self-worship.

Paul's depiction of the first and second Adams draws these two alternative theologies of significance and security into sharp relief. In

---

[61] In most modern translations *eikōn* in Rom. 1:23 is rendered as 'image' rather than 'idol', though the context clearly views it pejoratively.

both Romans 5 and 1 Corinthians 15 the apostle asserts important analogies between Adam and Christ, while also being quick to describe their critical differences. The Adam–Christ typology clarifies the manner in which the language of *eikōn* functions as a descriptor of the Creator–creature relation.

The Adam–Christ typology carried at its core the contrasting life–death and death–life cycles. Adam became a living being from the dust. Christ became a life-giving spirit (1 Cor. 15:45). By Adam's act of disobedience death was introduced (Rom. 5:15). By Christ's act of obedience the free gift of justification was introduced (Rom. 5:16). In Adam death descended upon all those in his image. In Christ new life is given to all those who bear his image (1 Cor. 15:49). Those who stand in solidarity with these two typological figures also stand in solidarity with their respective life and death cycles (1 Cor. 15:48).

Adam's test in the garden also connects him typologically with the testing of Jesus in the wilderness.[62] Christ is driven into the wilderness by the Spirit of God, a canonical means to assert that this is a divinely intended mission, though he stands in isolation in the wilderness. He has recently undergone the baptism of John, the canonical means of asserting that he identifies with all those in need of repentance. These two 'signs' connect him inextricably both to YHWH and to Adam.

The early chapters of Genesis represent the Adamic test occurring in the company of Eve. Jesus' test occurs in isolation. The Adamic test occurs in the lushness of the garden. Christ's test occurs in the desert. Adam is given every tree save one with which to feed himself. Christ fasts for forty days. The correspondingly contrasting contexts of the tests leads the reader to connect the two temptation narratives.[63]

The theological patterns of the two tests are also strikingly similar in their differences. Under interrogation by Satan Jesus is asked, 'If

---

[62] Luke's account of the temptation narrative of Jesus (Luke 4:1–12) is particularly relevant since Luke's genealogy of Jesus immediately preceding the temptation narrative places Jesus in the line of Adam (Luke 3:38).

[63] The fact that Jesus cites from Deut. 6 and 8 also strongly suggests that Israel's testing in the Sinai serves as a narrative link between Adam and Jesus. Both of these chapters narrate Israel's tests in the wilderness. Israel fails the test in the wilderness as did Adam in the garden. Adam is both banished from the garden and from the divine protections after his disobedience. The generation of Israel that disobeys in the desert is analogously refused entrance to the Promised Land, even as the divine Presence is taken away from them in the aftermath of the golden calf episode.

you are the Son of God, command this stone to become bread.' In the context of the preceding episode of Jesus' being baptized with the Spirit and being told by his Father that he is the beloved son in whom the Father is well pleased, Satan's words challenge the veracity of the divine word. In parallel fashion Adam and Eve were representatively asked by the serpent whether the divine prohibition against eating of the trees was to be taken with trust.

The first phase of the temptations is followed by a more direct assault on divine prerogatives. Satan seeks to strike a bargain with Jesus. If he worships Satan, in return Satan will give him all the kingdoms on earth. Jesus' response exposes Satan's bargain for its naked grasp for power. God alone is to be worshipped, the implicit assumption being that God alone is the Creator of all that is, and so all honour and worship belong to him. There are no realms over which divine authority does not rest. In corresponding fashion the serpent starkly asserts to Adam and Eve that if they eat of the tree they will be 'as God'. They will determine good and evil for themselves and thereby usurp the divine prerogative.

The final phase of the temptation narratives also draws out the correspondences. Adam and Eve are confronted in the final step not by any words of the serpent, but by the desires of their own hearts. It is the eyes through which the final phase of the temptation comes to them. They look at the tree and it is a delight to their eyes. And so they eat. The corresponding contrast with Jesus is striking. Satan tempts Jesus in the final phase by an appeal to the Scriptures that promises the divine protection of the Messiah. Satan tells Jesus to test God by throwing himself down from the pinnacle of the temple. Jesus responds by asserting that the divine promise was not given in order to be tested according to ordinary whims and desires. The test rather was to restrain human desires in accord with divine promises.

Paul's account of the Adam–Christ typology follows on from these correspondingly contrasting narratives of temptation. Adam is given life by God, but, in asserting independence from God, introduces death into the human experience. Jesus is the one who gives life in the first instance, but does not regard his divine right to life as something to be nakedly asserted. Rather he humbles himself, and by his act of righteousness brings life to many. By contrast Adam's representative act brings condemnation to all. Whereas the pattern of Adam is life followed by death, in Jesus the pattern inverts to death followed by life.

Being in the image of the image

After Paul draws out the Adam–Christ typology in Romans 5, he argues in Romans 6 that identifying with Christ in his death will also result in being identified with him in his resurrection. Those who are baptized into Christ's suffering and death will also be baptized into his resurrection. Then, in Romans 8, Paul claims that to share in being conformed to the image of the Son is to share in the death and resurrection pattern instituted and constituted by Jesus. Sharing the image of the one who is the image of God is to participate in his death and resurrection.[64] This identification with the pattern (image) of Christ's death and resurrection is nothing less than the gospel in summary form.[65]

The gospel finds itself in seed form, then, all the way back in Genesis 1 when God created humankind in the divine image. As the perfect image, Christ completes the original vocation of humankind and thereby shows humankind who they were originally intended to be.[66] This does not happen, however, without experiencing the cross wherein the power of the idols was broken and death lost its sting. The perfect image not only reveals what redeemed humans will eschatologically be but also loosens the bonds of their present enslavement to the idols they have created.

Being in the image of the image entails a new identity. Parts of the old identity persist until the final consummation, but with the coming of the perfect image the renewing project has begun. The New Testament has a variety of ways of speaking of the new identity – sometimes as a new self (Eph. 4:24; Col. 3:1, 10),[67] a new name (Rev. 3:12), a new future (John 14:3–4; Eph. 1:11) or a new age (Mark 10:30; Luke 18:30; Heb. 6:5). All of these bear witness to the reality that the old is fading while the new has not yet reached completion. While still

---

[64] Calvin (1960: 1.15.4) writes, 'if we are conformed to Christ's image, we are so restored that with true piety, righteousness, purity and intelligence we bear God's image'.

[65] Rowe (2005: 303) points at the striking difference between Paul's (negative) use of *eikōn* in Rom. 1 and his (positive) use of it in Rom. 8. He rightly suggests the difference is the object imaged in these diverse contexts. In the former instance it is the gods that do not exist. In the latter it is the living Christ.

[66] Grenz 2004: 617–628.

[67] Kline (1980: 54) notes, 'in the midst of the description of Revelation 22:4 of the glorified covenant community, renewed after the image of the Lord, it is said "they will see his face and his name will be in their foreheads." To say that the overcomers in the New Jerusalem bear the name of Christ on their forehead is to say that they reflect the glory of Christ which is to say that they bear the image of the glorified Christ.'

bearing the old image, Paul's promise is that 'we shall also bear the image of the man of heaven' (1 Cor. 15:49). It is the proverbial future breaking into the present.

One further important corollary of Paul's use of *eikōn* is that being in the image of the image is primarily manifested in communal contexts. It is idolatry by which the self becomes selfish. Putting on the new self is about treating others with respect, not showing partiality, not lying to them and not discriminating between Greek and Jew or between slave and free (Col. 3:5–11). Being 'in Christ' bears the fruit of recognizing that all who belong to Christ are members who all belong to each other.[68]

The claim that Jesus is the image of the invisible God in Colossians 1 is followed by the description in Colossians 3 that Christ is the very life of the church, and that the ecclesial community thereby is the image of Christ. The church now makes visible that which will only later become visible in Christ at the eschaton. So likewise in 2 Corinthians 3 Paul asserts that in the church's gaze upon the face of Christ they are being renewed after his image from one degree of glory to another. It is not until 2 Corinthians 4 that Paul reveals that the next order of glory into which the church is being renewed is the eschatological glory of Christ's resurrected life.[69] The church bearing the image of Christ (2 Cor. 3:18) is derived from Christ who bears the image of God (2 Cor. 4:4).

The idolatries of the self that so strongly tempted the Corinthian churches were viewed as normative by the Gentile culture that surrounded them. But it was a common charge in the first century for the church to be indicted on the charge of atheism and idolatries of their own. In refusing to pay due honour to the local deities that protected the city they were suspected of inventing their own gods to

---

[68] The church is the fundamental context in which the image of Christ is manifested on this side of eternity. It is the community of God's people who, in their fidelity to Christ and to each other, bear the imprint of Christ. In a highly democratized environment such as the present, this stands as a necessary corrective to the temptations towards forms of piety that are strikingly individualistic. In different cultural settings where communal hierarchies are in place the temptations towards passive pieties may well be stronger. But the greater temptations today veer undoubtedly towards the privacy and convenience of each individual as the centre of all choices.

[69] So Horton (2005: 112) writes, 'The glorification already partly realized in the possession of the Holy Spirit as a down payment, will be the full investiture of each believer "male and female" as royal "son". This may be why Paul (Rom. 8:18–25) puts an eschatological spin on adoption, deferring its full accomplishment until the whole creation is able to participate with redeemed humanity in the Sabbath enthronement of God.'

serve their own needs. As a consequence Christians were viewed with deep suspicion.

It seems likely that Paul's juxtaposition of idol terminology through-out his writing with the 'one God, one Lord' formula is not coincidental but deliberately intended because of the apparent paradoxical and potentially scandalous nature of the Christian proclamation of Jesus' lordship. If the worship of another human is idolatrous, why would the worship of Jesus be any different? This was a strong and recurring indictment made by Jews of Christians in the first century. Paul argues that Christians are not guilty of idolatry in worshipping Jesus, because Jesus is not a deity separate from the one God but rather the latter's image in the creation and restoration of the world.[70] This solution to the 'multiple gods in heaven' problem is similar to that in the Gospel of John, where Jesus reinterprets the Shema as being compatible with the coinherence of the Father and the Son, because the two are 'one' (John 10:30; 17:11, 22–23).

In the next chapter we turn to a surprising reappearance of this indictment of idolatry levelled at Christians in the nineteenth century. It was focused not merely on the person of Jesus, but on the wider claim that all religious loyalties are fundamentally forms of idolatry in so far as they underwrite the project of creating a god in human likeness. It was a challenge that illuminated the remarkable conceptual power of idolatry, and also shook Christianity to the core in the Western world. It is an episode worth revisiting with a new set of lenses.

---

[70] Marcus 2006: 152–164.

Chapter Seven

The rise of suspicion: the religious criticism of religion

'Idolatry' is perhaps the one religious category that has taken on and maintains the most secular and critical power.
(Batnitzky 2000: 3)

Idolatry as ideological criticism: the stage is set

In the hands of the Old Testament prophets idolatry was as powerful a warning against false religion as could be imagined. Until the nineteenth century it would have been almost unthinkable that idolatry could be used against not only false religion but against religion itself. What may at first seem an odd use of idolatry as a diatribe against Christian faith in the hands of the great secular prophets of the nineteenth century in fact turns out to be a powerful reminder of the theological temptations that befall the human heart in all ages. It should also come as no surprise that Christianity's sharpest critics at the end of the Enlightenment should rail against the established church in much the same fashion that the Old Testament prophets railed against Israel's idolatries in the seventh and eighth centuries BC. The surprise in the nineteenth century was that this form of criticism withered away almost as quickly as it arose. Narrating the story of the secular prophets in the nineteenth century illuminates both the conceptual power of idolatry and the enduring liturgical nature of human identity.

The nineteenth century is neatly demarcated by two of the greatest minds of the modern era: Immanuel Kant (1724–1804) at the beginning and Friedrich Nietzsche (1844–1900) at the end. It is imperative to note that Kant's intellectual shadow dominated the agenda of the nineteenth century unlike any thinker has dominated an age before or since. At the other end of the century it is not an exaggeration to claim that Nietzsche brought the Kantian enterprise to a close, though there were signs that it lingered on for another fifty years, albeit in a severely weakened form.

Alfred North Whitehead wrote famously of the history of philosophy that it was but a footnote to Plato. How much more, then, is it true to say that the nineteenth century was but a footnote to Immanuel Kant. No figure of any age so dominated philosophical discourse in the succeeding age as Kant. His shadow was long and his influence pervasive in the nineteenth century. Nearly every thinker of consequence in the nineteenth century thought Kant had set the agenda to which serious public intellectuals had to respond.

Kant was the central figure of the German Enlightenment. He was born, raised and spent most of his life in the East Prussian city of Königsberg (Kaliningrad). By his own admission there was little of note in Kant's biography. He led a dull life. He never married and the well-rehearsed story is told of the housewives of Königsberg setting their clocks by the regularity of Kant's walks in the afternoon. He was raised in a deeply religious home, studied theology in the university, but was generally impatient with traditional formulations of religious belief. He also had an abiding distrust of history as the primary vehicle of religious truth. Being faithful to his own Pietist background, Kant attempted to safeguard religious belief from the inroads being made by a rationalist scepticism grounded in historical criticism. He believed traditional Christian confession was little prepared for this onslaught.

Kant's central project through the productive years of his writing career concerned the grounding of the natural sciences in a critical philosophical framework that was influenced by both the empirical and rationalist traditions. He affirms in his first major work, *The Critique of Pure Reason* (1781), that human knowledge begins with sense impressions (following David Hume) but has to consist of more than mere sense impressions. There must be a natural ordering of the impressions according to certain mental categories, such as the concepts of space and time. These categories are the filters through which the world is apprehended and interpreted. They also provide the glue that holds the impressions of the world together.

There are objects that cannot be filtered through our mental categories, most notably God and the self. These are objects of the noumenal realm. They are not the sorts of things of which we can form any sense impression. Try as we might, God and the self cannot be seen or touched. Consequently Kant believed they were not objects of knowledge, but rather objects of faith. Convictions about them rest not on any empirical evidence, but rather on their utility for ethical conduct. In matters of morality Kant thought the concepts of justice and goodness were universal. But further, he believed, our concepts of them depended on there being a final standard of justice and goodness, namely God. Kant rejected the classical proofs for God's existence and in their stead argued on the basis of morality that humankind nonetheless had to continue to believe in God if morality were to survive.

Kant was convinced that knowledge was best pursued outside the bounds of the authority of church and state. He defended this claim in his aptly titled work *Religion Within the Bound of Reason* (1793). He believed that an officer of the church was not free to teach what he pleased. It was his religious duty to teach what the church taught. A scholar on the other hand ought to have the freedom to follow truth wherever it led. As a scholar, empirical and rational evidence were paramount to sustain conviction. In matters of religion simple faith alone could sustain belief. But in matters of science and history reason was humankind's only reliable guide.

The Enlightenment challenge to older forms of institutional authority was by the opening of the nineteenth century well entrenched.[1] Kant brought these challenges together into a sophisticated conceptual framework that gave intelligible voice to the suspicion of all cultural authorities except an individual's own reason. The external authorities, most notably of church and king, were replaced by a new subjective authority – critical human reason, as Kant had described its inner workings. This effectively formalized what has often been called the 'subjective turn'.[2] The individual subject (or at least those individual subjects who happened to be teaching in prestigious universities of Europe) was seen as the pre-eminent authority in matters pertaining to the constituents of the real world and how that world was known. The working assumption was that a disinterested scholar, rather than any religious cleric, was in a far superior position to know the world as it really was.

[1] Griffin (1989a: 1–8; 29–62) suggests that the heart of the Enlightenment lay in its claim that the supernatural God, the God of traditional Western (Augustinian) Christian theology, has died. The rejection of the fundamental authority of God then entails the rejection of other institutional forms of authority such as the church and the king.

[2] See the generally critical account of the 'subjective turn' in Stout 1981. An interpretative essay with a concern for the larger social implications is May 1976. Standard histories of philosophy normally see the 'subjective turn' as the explanatory key for understanding modern philosophy, starting with René Descartes in the sixteenth century. See Copleston 1993a. See also the highly influential set of essays gathered in the collection Rorty 1967, which charts the extension of the 'subjective turn' in the twentieth century in the form of a 'linguistic turn'.

According to Kant, ecclesiastical commitment clouded one's view of reality.

This precipitated a crisis throughout the nineteenth century regarding the proper grounds for believing in God. The long shadow Kant's work exerted on the nineteenth century suggested that religion could no longer be grounded in historical facts or abstract metaphysical claims. One very compelling alternative was to look for the origin of religion within the psychological needs of humans themselves. This alternative supposed that scholars ought to pay attention to the natural origins of religion, that is those elements of human nature that gave rise to religious belief. The search for these naturalized origins took nineteenth-century thinkers in many directions, though they were bound together by the belief that religion's source was not in the historical and verifiable past nor in a transcendental and absolute future. Religion belonged to the inner emotive (and non-rational) nature of humans.

The significance of Kant's legacy in the nineteenth century was effectively to divide intellectual enquiry into two separate domains, the secular and the sacred. The secular world of science was the world of facts and data. The sacred world of religion was the world of faith and trust. In the one realm objectivity and hard-headed scepticism were prized; in the other, blind belief and obedience to authority ruled. There was virtually no interaction between these two domains, nor, according to Kant, should that be worrisome. To hard-headed sceptics after Kant the task was less to defend the secular domains of knowledge than to wonder aloud why the sacred world would any longer be needed. Though it did not appear so at the time, the nineteenth century witnessed the virtual explosion of the secular expanse and the compartmentalization of the sacred realm. Throughout the nineteenth century secular prophets foretold a day when the secular would entirely swallow the sacred, and there would no longer reside a compelling reason to believe in the old world of transcendent beings and traditional values.

The intellectual momentum throughout the nineteenth century headed in the direction of religious unbelief, though much of that did not appear in the English-speaking world until the beginning of the twentieth century.[3] The major intellectual voices mostly spoke German in the nineteenth century and pressed the divide between the

---

[3] The rise of logical positivism in the 1920s was a major turning point in the English-speaking world in switching the burden of proof from atheism to theism. Two recent sympathetic histories are Stadler 2001 and Friedman 1999.

secular and the sacred in a fashion probably unforseen by Kant.[4] Starting with Ludwig Feuerbach and culminating in Friedrich Nietzsche, the secular so expanded as to make the sacred seem virtually irrelevant. Traditional religious belief was on trial and a guilty verdict seemed assured by the tone of the secular prophets.

Kant had argued at the end of *The Critique of Pure Reason* that the objects of the noumenal world (God and self most prominently) were objects not of knowledge, but rather of faith. The secular prophets of the nineteenth century accepted this premise, but instead of viewing the objects of faith as protected from the inroads of empirical enquiry (as the nineteenth-century transcendentalists claimed) they viewed them as irrelevant and in many instances as damaging to human progress. After Kant (and Hegel) these radical thinkers wondered aloud why people believed in God if there was no empirical evidence in his favour. They also well understood the intricacies of the Christian tradition, since most of them had been reared in it. Borrowing the most powerful form of criticism against false religion, the secular prophets turned the tool on its head. Instead of seeking the grounds of false beliefs in idolatry, they supposed religious belief of every kind was intrinsically idolatrous. It was idolatrous precisely because it manifested the disposition of all religious people to create a god in their own image. Religion and idolatry went hand in hand because they were identical – or so the secular prophets hoped to prove.

Kant's primary interlocutor early in the nineteenth century was G. W. F. Hegel, who accepted some of Kant's critical realism but also thought it profoundly insensitive to larger metaphysical realities.[5] In many ways Hegel thought he might be able to turn the clock back – reversing the trends unleashed by Kant and the shift towards empirical investigations. Hegel was one of the last grand metaphysicians of the era and in enigmatic ways provided a perfect foil for the later radical secular prophets to appropriate Kant for their own purposes. As it turned out, most German radical intellectuals of the nineteenth century saw Hegel as the last gasp of an outdated, outmoded religion – the religion that believed in things that could not be seen or heard.

[4] Recent revisionist histories of Kant strongly suggest that his primary intention was not merely to salvage some limited space for religious belief in the era of early modern science but to make religious faith more credible as the very means that could give transcendental coherence to the project of science in the first place. See Ameriks 2012 and Hare 2009.

[5] A helpful survey of recent Hegel scholarship can be found in Moyer and Quante 2011.

A quick detour through Hegel is needed to set the wider context for the introduction of idolatry as the prime conceptual tool in the project of the radical secular prophets.

A central Hegelian theme was the contention that history had an ultimate purpose, grounded in the outworking of the Absolute Mind.[6] History moved in inexorable fashion as the self-actualization of this Absolute Mind. In other words, ideas moved history. In religion Hegel supposed that animism was the earliest world view, opposed at some later point by pantheism. A resulting synthesis of sorts, polytheism was itself later opposed by theism. Theism persisted for a time until it clashed with deism, and the resulting synthesis was Hegel's own brand of religious idealism. It was this synthesis that Hegel believed had brought the dialectical movement of religious history to a climax. This cycle of conflicting religious world views was neither haphazard nor accidental.[7] Neither could that history be reduced merely to empirical and circumstantial realities. It was ideologies rather than social and material realities that mattered most.

Hegel's religious views were an enigmatic blend of Platonism and Christianity. Plato had supposed that the purpose and meaning of objects in the world lay in a world beyond history. Christianity supposed that the purpose and meaning of objects in the world lay in the meaning granted them by a transcendent deity. Hegel combined the two by collapsing the transcendent world and the historical realm into one.

His followers divided into two camps: those who believed his system was compatible with Christianity (right-wing Hegelians) and those who did not believe this (left-wing Hegelians). The vastly more influential left-wing Hegelians sought to press the radical demands of history as they perceived them on any and all ideology, especially religious ideologies. In part they reversed the priority of ideas over history that Hegel had thought so critical. Rather than ideas moving history, the radicals supposed that concrete empirical history was the only source of ideas. The left-wing Hegelians included biblical scholars such as D. F. Strauss and F. C. Baur, who sought to undermine the ancient conviction that the Bible was a word from outside history. They argued that the Bible was merely a product of its own historical contexts. Other left-wing Hegelians such as Ludwig Feuerbach and

---

[6] Earlier generations might have referred to the Absolute Mind as God, but Hegel (1807) believed that granting Absolute Mind a name reduced the metaphysical ground of all being merely to a humanized deity.

[7] Lewis 2011: 192–209.

Karl Marx claimed that all convictions about God were in fact merely disguised assertions about humanity. In their hands theology became anthropology. These radicals followed Hegel in supposing that history was always a struggle. Religious, political and social conflict were at the very centre of human history. Far from trying to achieve a state of perfection, real social science ought to study and validate these historical tensions, and across the breadth of the nineteenth century religion was often viewed as a primary animating source of conflict. This stereotyping of religion and historical conflict would last throughout the nineteenth century. And the reason it lasted, in part, was that it provided a 'clean' alternative to Christian views of God's providence over history. It appeared to provide a safely secular way to explain history.

Idolatry as psychological projection

Christianity's radical critics in the nineteenth century emerged in a most surprising way. Using a fundamental argument against false religion as the primary argument against all religion had very little historical precedent. The expectations in the conflict between Christianity and its nineteenth-century detractors would more likely have focused on the accepted facts of history. Was the resurrection historical fact or not? Did miracles happen or not? These oft-heard questions of the eighteenth century receded into the background by the early part of the nineteenth century in large measure because religion had been reconceived primarily as a matter of the heart, a place where the facts of history did not encroach. Far from safeguarding religious faith, this opened it up to an entirely different line of attack. That attack began most clearly in the work of Ludwig Feuerbach, the best known of the left-wing Hegelians and one of their most radical. He had studied at the University of Heidelberg and then at Berlin under Hegel himself. His first published work in 1830 was a searing criticism of Christianity, painting it to be inhuman and egotistic.[8] Before long he was widely known for his zeal for atheism, a zeal that probably cost him a permanent appointment as a university professor in Germany,

[8] *Thoughts on Death and Immortality* (1981) was published anonymously by Feuerbach, and effectively ended his academic career because of its biting satire and vitriol articulated against the history of Christianity. Though it seems incredible today that an atheist would lose an academic post because of such criticism, the pervasive Pietism in the German universities of the early nineteenth century simply could not tolerate the intensity of Feuerbach's anti-Christian rhetoric.

but it was also a zeal for which the twentieth century viewed him as prophetic. Feuerbach's overriding aim was to undermine the confidence in a divine being whom he believed did not exist. Feuerbach did not suppose that the Christian church was particularly detrimental to civilization. Christians had simply misplaced a trust they ought to have had in themselves for a loyalty to a non-existent deity. At times he supposed the church was the last remnant of superstition left in the West, but the church still possessed an unfortunate hold on Western culture. His task was not so much to destroy the church as to cleanse it of superstitions. Karl Barth would later write of Feuerbach:

> His principal aim was to change the friends of God into the friends of man, believers into thinkers, worshippers into workers, candidates for the other world into students of this world, Christians, who on their own confession are half-animal and half-angel into men – whole men.[9]

Feuerbach believed the Christian religion confessed loyalty to a being that did not exist. This meant that in the study of religion scholars learned about the religious yearnings of human beings, not about some transcendent reality. Those religious yearnings might have been perfectly natural but were misplaced when viewed as being fulfilled by a deity residing in a distant place in the sky. Feuerbach's task was to reorient the religious impulse from a worship of an external object to the admiration of the aspirations of all humankind.

Humans, he believed, were prone to create God in their own image as a projection of their ideals. The problem lay in trusting the ideal as if it existed independent of one's desires. The ideal might have been useful as an imaginative construct to illuminate fundamental values, but the objectification of the concept was dangerous. Feuerbach contended that the creation of God as an objectified ideal alienated human beings from their own nature.

Lying behind this prophetic warning was his conviction that self-consciousness was both a great glory and a great danger. Self-consciousness separated humankind from the beasts and permitted civilization to emerge. But it also prompted the creation of idols. The ability to name oneself as a species (in contrast to the animals) led to the illusion that abstract objects such as 'goodness', 'god' or

---

[9] Barth 1957: x.

'humankind' existed above individual human beings. Concepts such as beauty or truth existed only as imaginative concepts in the mind. This entailed for Feuerbach that there was no ideal human by any name – much less a deity that existed in a human image. There were only concrete human beings. In Feuerbach's wonderfully ugly phrase, 'Man is what he eats,' nothing more. Combining all of the positive character traits of individual humans gave rise to believing in a perfect human character, which came to be known by the name 'God'. To see this was to be cured of it Feuerbach thought. The hard part, however, was seeing it. And what better way for Christians to see this, thought Feuerbach, than to reframe the language of idolatry. Feuerbach well understood that the Old Testament prophets had charged Israel with believing in false gods, of creating gods in their own image. Prophets such as Isaiah and Amos understood the powerful human drive to craft a deity that served selfish interests. What these prophets failed to recognize, according to Feuerbach, was that YHWH was Israel's original idol, created in the image of the powerful overlord who would protect them against the tyrants of the ancient world, and provide for them a Promised Land. Railing against the idols of pagans, Israel had failed to see their own idolatry.

All gods were simply the objectification of human aspirations. 'What humans are not, but what they will to be, just that and only that is God.'[10] Humans hope for peace and so create a God who will bring peace. Humans hope for love, and so create a God of love. Humans hope for victory, and so create a God who will bring them victory. Humans create a God in the mirror of their hopes. 'If God were a being of the birds, he would have been a winged creature' (28).

An idol symbolized a God who did not exist. But the power of the idol was nonetheless profound and often enduring. In the modern world the gods of ancient Greece had come to be viewed as fictional figures in mythical stories. But at one time these ancient deities demanded absolute loyalty from their human subjects. Some gods demanded children to be sacrificed to them. Others demanded ritual prostitution to be performed. Ancient city states were powerful precisely because their local gods were powerful, or so the ancients believed. So it was with Christianity, Feuerbach believed.

When the ancient polytheistic civilizations fell, they were replaced by a Roman empire that united much of the known world. No longer could they be content with local deities. Rome's god must eventually

---

[10] Feuerbach 1957: 24.

be shown to be universal and absolute. Their culture and context demanded a monotheism, and what better place to look than to ancient Israel, yet not in its original Semitic context but in its reshaped Hellenized form, namely that of Christianity.[11] The Romans borrowed Christianity as the ideological means to justify themselves and their place in the world. Long gone, however, in the nineteenth century was the Roman ideology in culture. The world was no longer Roman, and if the Enlightenment had accomplished anything it was to unsettle the old Roman alliance between throne and altar. Political authority rested in the voice of the populace, not in the mediated divine voice of the church. Political culture had begun to loose its bonds to monarchies and must now be freed from Roman religious idols as well. Feuerbach did not desire a new replacement set of idols but the removal of all idols. He desired a culture that simply believed in itself.

The process of overcoming the idols of religion would be a long and arduous task. Idols were the sorts of things people grew comfortable with, which could not be given up easily. The way out of idolatry was first to look inside the human heart itself, to see the needs that gave rise to creating idols in the first place. If those needs could be exposed as the source of religious belief, then it would not be long before the edifice built upon those foundations would come crumbling down. Feuerbach referred to this as the 'psychogenetic method'. Locating the psychological origins of belief effectively undermined its validity.

God had to cease to exist independently of human hopes and desires. The proper object of religious worship was in fact humankind. It was important to locate the essence of perfection not outside human experience but within humans themselves. This would change the worship of God into the worship of humankind. It would also place squarely on the shoulders of humankind the responsibility to work for peace, to show love – to exhibit the very characteristics they had mistakenly projected upon God. Humans needed to exert their own will rather than to believe that someone or something else would or could solve their problems.

---

[11] Apart from the fact that Feuerbach's historical argument had no evidence in its favour, his contention did have a kind of simple elegance in its explanatory power. It was this 'alternative explanatory framework' that provided justification for greater freedom for secularists from ecclesiastical control. This note of liberation had been sounded in the Enlightenment, and continued unabated among the secular prophets of the nineteenth century. See Harvey 1995.

To this end, then, Feuerbach attempted to translate Christianity into a language without any transcendent entities, without any gods. In calculating fashion he believed he could rid the world of idolatry by translating the historic Christian confession into a language without theological overtones. He wrote of performing 'pneumatic hydrotherapy' – by which he meant throwing out the baptismal water and replacing it with real water.[12] Humans needed to be rid of the magical water, and get about the business of cleaning themselves with real water. Feuerbach hoped the sacred would get translated into a fully secular discourse.

A brief critical note ought to be sounded now with regard to Feuerbach, as he set the agenda for other secular prophets throughout the nineteenth century. Like many of his contemporaries Feuerbach had yet to wrestle with radical evil, and in particular with radical social evil. He expressed a naive optimism about unbridled human progress freed from the religious constraints of the past. Later thinkers in the left-wing Hegelian tradition would try to do greater justice to evil though there remained a residue of genuine naiveté towards evil. Without God there was no final constraint on evil, as the twentieth century all too painfully bore out.

If Feuerbach had a naively optimistic view of humankind, he also had no means to account for his own views. He believed in human goodness but had no ultimate ground for it. Human dignity in hindsight appeared as but a remnant Feuerbach borrowed from his own prior Judeo-Christian tradition, though without any borrowing rights! After Feuerbach it became the task to ground human dignity in something intrinsic to human culture, though this remained fragile given the transitory character of that culture.

Without recognizing it, Feuerbach had given an implicit counterargument to his claims. Maybe unbelief also had a psychological explanation that in turn would undermine its validity. We follow the narrative from Feuerbach to Marx to Freud to Nietzsche before this irony fully unfolded.

Idolatry as alienation and oppression

Like Feuerbach Marx was well acquainted with the Judeo-Christian tradition. He was born of Prussian-Jewish parents, who converted to Protestantism for what appeared matters of convenience. Though

[12] Feuerbach 1957: 236.

young Karl was baptized into the Christian church, he was never religiously serious and was always suspicious of the motivations behind religious commitment. He studied law and philosophy at university and was, like Feuerbach, profoundly influenced by Hegel. He was arrested, tried and expelled from Germany in 1848 for publishing a radical journal of political protest, and lived the rest of his life in London in relative poverty. During his early time in London he met Friedrich Engels, a prosperous textile mill owner who would support Marx for much of his life.

Marx was taken aback by the extreme working conditions of the early stages of the Industrial Revolution in England. Having none of the naive optimism of Feuerbach regarding human nature, he was appalled at the inhumanity so manifest throughout the Industrial Revolution. Ordinary workers in the factories were exploited with tedious menial labour, low wages and painfully long hours. Young children were forced into similar conditions as the only means of support for their families. They were often given barely enough food to sustain their existence. Workers were treated as commodities. The intensity of factory life crushed many of the labourers in its grip. Jobs were scarce and pay minimal. Demand for jobs was greater than their supply. As a result owners were permitted to abuse workers as they saw fit. For all intents and purposes workers had become virtual slaves of owners.

Following Feuerbach, Marx thought humans were simply the matter out of which they had come. But unlike Feuerbach, Marx thought rather pessimistically about human nature left to itself. Humans were intrinsically selfish apart from the social pressures to sacrifice themselves for the good of their community. Social networks exerted inordinate pressure on individuals to conform to acceptable moral standards, and Marx supposed these social networks were rooted primarily in religious ways of life. If one could change the religious social structures, then there would be hope of changing individuals.

Firmly within the Hegelian tradition Marx supposed that conflict lay near the centre of human history and was the force that pushed it forward. For Marx progress was inevitable but could be accomplished only through struggle. That struggle was best described in terms of social conflict between diverse economic classes. And that struggle could be best understood by more carefully understanding human nature. Marx believed it was of the essence of human nature to work, and humans had an intrinsic natural value that was simply a function of being human. They also possessed an exchange value that was their value as determined by the economic system in which they laboured. A farmer was of much value in an agrarian society, and a banker of much value in an early capitalist society. Updating the illustration, rock stars are valuable today only in an entertainment culture.

Workers could be exploited when their exchange value was itself controlled by individuals seeking their own good rather than the good of the whole community. Deviant social organizations as well as individuals would exploit workers if given the opportunity, as was happening throughout England during the early days of the Industrial Revolution. The result was that workers were alienated from their own labour, neither controlling its value nor its conditions. Craftsmen were alienated from the products of their labours on the assembly line, becoming cogs in a machine they did not own. The drudgery and tedious work further alienated workers from their dignity. Lying behind this dehumanizing and degrading system were the owners of the factories and the religious institutions that legitimated their oppression.

As the emerging dominant economic system of the nineteenth century, capitalism was most often justified by appeal to religious grounds in general and to Christianity in particular. For Marx the Judeo-Christian religion was capitalism's legitimating world view. Capitalism had latched onto it as the means to validate it. To use Marx's famous phrase, religion had become the 'opium of the people', a drug needed to keep the addictions to capitalism strong. Religion was the sentiment of a heartless world and the soul of a soulless condition.[13]

For Marx the use of religion to validate the power structures during the Industrial Revolution revealed its authentic character as a determined oppressor. A God created in the oppressor's image was nothing but a fantasy figure serving to justify the system. In capitalism this 'God' preached obedience to masters, humility and meekness in the face of hardship and, above all, rewards in another life. All of these religious 'virtues' encouraged workers to be servile to those in authority.

For Marx the criticism of religion was the beginning of the end of oppression and alienation. If religion was fundamentally idolatrous, creating a God to serve the economic interests of masters, then

---

[13] This phrase is borrowed from Westphal in one of the best treatments of Marx's critique of religion (1994).

workers would have to throw off the shackles of religion if they genuinely desired freedom and dignity. Religion might have appeared to give hope in a hopeless world, but that hope had to be made more concrete and historical and could be done so only by the abolition of religion and the revolt of the workers against their oppressors. For the owners, religion helped to cement the status quo. For the workers, it helped them cope with the status quo. In both cases religion was a conserving force on behalf of the status quo. For Marx the only way forward was the unmasking of these idols. That would be accomplished only by a determined revolt against capitalism and exploitation, by throwing off the shackles of religion in favour of an atheistic humanism. Until humans believed in themselves they would not throw off the burdens of their oppressors.

Marx's antidote to capitalism was found in his most influential work, *The Communist Manifesto*. In that work he laid out a programme whereby private property was to be abolished, religion to be abandoned and human communities to flourish. It assumed that without capitalist economic structures mutual cooperation would emerge among communities and even nations. Goods would be produced according to ability and distributed according to need.

Marx's vision was thoroughly utopian and, with the hindsight of the twentieth century, incredibly naive. It did not take individual evil seriously, hoping only that systemic changes would produce the eradication of evil altogether. And, unbeknown to Marx, communities could oppress as easily as individuals. However, lest Marx's critique be too easily dismissed, we should note that Amos sounded similar alarms about the oppression within Israel during the eighth century BC. In like manner James, in the first century AD, brought attention to the manner in which religion could be reshaped to serve the interests of the rich and powerful. Marx's critical use of idolatry worked because greed and oppression often had a religious face to them. Christians were (are) not immune to using their own religious views to legitimate actions repugnant to the gospel. Marx understood that better than much of the established church in the nineteenth century.

What he did not so easily see was that religious confession may also function as a prophetic balance against human injustice because it offers a Word from outside. Its transcendent voice stands as a judge over all peoples and thereby offers the very tools of culture criticism for which Marx yearned. One need only read the Old Testament prophets to find this. Without a transcendent Word the only judge of human actions can come from within human cultures, which by all accounts are always corruptible, individually and corporately.

Idolatry and the origin of religion

Placing Freud in the chronological sequence of the nineteenth-century secular prophets is stretching the temporal construct almost to the breaking point. Freud belongs most fully to the twentieth century and most assuredly was neither a philosopher nor a theologian. However, there is no clearer representative of the flowering of the secular prophets than in the work of Freud. He distilled their larger claims into a working framework that would be influential well beyond the midpoint of the twentieth century. And though Freud's primary frame of reference was psychology, his impact was felt most acutely across the religious spectrum. His treatment of the natural neurosis of religion brought the secular prophets' tradition to its most aggressive posture.

Leaving aside Freud's developed thought on psychological structures, his central contribution to the discourse on idolatry lay in his psychological depictions of the rise of religion. For Freud religion was a psychological disorder common to humankind. Religion arose because of an inner conflict within each person. This was a conflict of dependence upon others and the yearning for independence from others. These were natural forces warring within each person's soul. The 'normal' state of this conflict depended upon one's own life journey. At birth each person was naturally more predisposed towards dependency on others for survival. As natural development took place, maturing individuals eventually reached a stage where they became self-reliant. Failure to work through that transition from dependence to independence resulted in neuroses of various kinds. When taken collectively, these neuroses expressed themselves most prominently in religious ways.

The central assumption of Freud was that religion has no hold on the 'way things are'. Religious claims about the existence of God ought to be dismissed because they have no basis in fact. The more pressing question is, why is there religion in the first place? Freud depicted a hypothetical ancient tribal context as the clearest way to explain the emergence of religion in society. The chief of the tribe was viewed as the primal father in the tribe. He held complete authority by virtue of his office as chief, largely justified by the need for order in a surrounding world of chaos. Those outside the structures of power eventually revolted against the chief simply because of the natural desire for independence. In their mutiny the chief would have been killed. However, far from being freed from the tyranny of authority, the younger warriors would have suffered a great sense of loss and guilt. The loss of leadership brought chaos and disruption. To repair the moral fabric that appeared to hold the tribe together the young murderers created a totemic religion wherein the memories of the dead chief restored order and meaning. The young warriors worshipped the chief as if he were still alive, creating representations of him out of wood and stone. It was not long before someone claimed that the chief was still alive, spiritually existing in some distant heaven. The projection of his image was identified as a supreme being and eventually referred to as God. The will of the chief became absolute and therein the warriors eventually found forgiveness.

This mythical depiction of Freud's described the collective 'Oedipal complex' from which religion was to be explained and explained away. Given the familial analogies within Christianity (Father and Son), Freud intended to discredit religious belief by claiming that it evoked a psychological dependence that all social scientists then regarded as neurotic – or so it seemed to Freud. The social structures built to support the myth of religion had been strong enough to sustain this totemic world view for several thousand years. With the coming of modernity Freud saw a time when the shackles of religion could be thrown off and humans could gain their (psychological) independence.

At the root of religion, then, was fear. It was the fear that one could not stand alone. It was a fear of the unknown – especially the unknowns of life in the face of natural disasters. Storms of immense power and natural forces beyond human control threatened human survival at every turn. The first step in dealing with these fears of the unknown was to attempt to tame nature itself. Freud supposed that early animists humanized nature by projecting spiritual qualities onto it. But when nature still seemed to treat humankind arbitrarily, tossing storms of destruction at them, a stronger solution had to be found. If nature could not be tamed, a supernatural force was needed. This supernatural force had to be powerful enough to control the threatening nature, and yet compassionate enough to care for those threatened by nature. Better still if that supernatural force were itself personal and had much in common with humankind. This would assure that the supernatural force would be loyal to the very humans threatened by the forces of nature. And so the resultant mechanism to overcome their fears was to create an idol in the image of those in need, yet stronger and cleverer than them. But far from granting them solace from their fears, this idol kept them in a perpetual state of dependence, always demanding obedience.

The failure to mature beyond the stage of dependence created the opportunity for religion. And religion all but guaranteed that humans would never achieve the independence for which they yearned. This Freudian diagnosis seemed irrefutable to a point. It offered no evidence that could contravene it. It depended simply on the explanatory power of its suggestions. Those who wanted to be freed from the constraints of religious authority had simply to cast away their shackles and be free. Recognizing the neurosis was the first step in curing it. A determined exercise of the will was the lone missing ingredient beyond the correct diagnosis.

The Freudian explanations of religion were fairly tidy. And like its predecessors, the explanations were conceptually dependent on biblical notions of idolatry. Biblical religion had offered resources that in turn could be (and were) used against it. The blind spot for this use of idolatry was the problem of self-referential incoherence. Any criticism of religion that depended finally upon a psychological depiction is open to the same charge. If there were corrupting motives behind religion, could not a similar tale be told with respect to the motives behind the critique? This is to argue that if there were a psychology of belief, there might also be a psychology of unbelief.[14] The presence (or absence) of psychological motives behind (ir)religious beliefs entailed neither the truth nor falsity of the beliefs in question. Freud, as the secular prophets had before him, assumed a naturalistic world view, and on that basis went looking for the only possible cause of religion – a natural one.

However, as with Marx so with Freud, one ought to be careful in too easily dismissing the naiveté of the criticism. The canon of Scripture is replete with examples of idolatrous beliefs and actions on the part of the visible covenant community of God. Woe unto the modern church if secular prophets are required to identify the modern forms of idolatry within Christendom. The church ought to be better equipped to think about itself critically in an age of great temptations. And in part a debt is owed to Freud for exposing tendencies of psychological dependence that often influence how God is viewed. In the present environment too often those dependencies mean that God's

---

[14] In a thoughtful but far too brief account Sproul (1974) turned the tables on the cultured despisers of nineteenth-century religion in just this manner.

primary responsibility is to look out for the wealth and well-being of the person. Is it not rather the responsibility of the church to reflect the living and true God in his desire for truth, beauty and justice? Religion can be psychologically manipulated and the danger in an individualist culture is precisely that at which Freud often pointed.

However, the secular prophets from Feuerbach to Freud little understood the character of God's holiness as portrayed in Scripture. Whereas the tamed god of civil religion might have been an easy target to shoot at, this was far less so in the case of the terrifying God met in the books of Job, Isaiah, Hebrews or Revelation – or almost any other of the canonical books if looked at carefully enough. When Job is overwhelmed in the face of God's presence, there can be little doubt that, left to his own devices, this is not the sort of God that Job would have created (Job 38 – 40). So with Isaiah's terrifying vision of the holiness of God, one would be hard pressed to conclude that YHWH is merely a figment of Isaiah's imagination, created to meet Isaiah's private needs. The author to the book of Hebrews well understood the costliness of salvation in Christ, and it cannot reasonably be said that this is a gospel he would have created if given the opportunity to make things easy for himself. So the suffering and martyrdom portrayed throughout the book of Revelation makes it highly unlikely that any person looking for comfort and convenience would have created a god that brought so much difficulty into the lives of his people. In these and so many other ways the biblical message resounds with a message too overwhelming to be simply a product of an idolatrous imagination. The church ought to be well reminded that in the face of the withering critiques of the secular prophets it must seek to recover the holiness of God in its fullness.

Friedrich Nietzsche (1844–1900)

No one saw the stark contrast between belief and unbelief as Nietzsche, and therefore no other of the secular prophets saw as clearly the implications of atheism. It is fair to say that Nietzsche was the last of the secular prophets, bringing this tradition to its conceptual end, and served as a loud reminder that atheism did not come without great cost. There was no room for easy belief nor easy unbelief after him. It is also important to note that he not only brought the tradition of the secular prophets to a close, but also foreshadowed the coming of the postmodern tradition that put to rest the easy confidence in human nature and rationality trumpeted by the Enlightenment.

Born in Prussian Saxony, Nietzsche's father was the latest in a long line of Lutheran pastors. But sadly Nietzsche's father died when Friedrich was just 5 years old, leaving a wife, his mother, two sisters and a daughter to care for the lone son. There was a history of sickness among the males in the family line, and Friedrich was no exception. A fragile child, he was often filled with melancholy and overcome by physical maladies. He battled with bouts of insanity in later life, and wrote his most profound works in a cryptic prose intended to confuse as much as clarify. He died at the relatively young age of 56.

Nietzsche was given a classical education and developed an early love for Greek poetry and mythology. His love of the ancient pagan authors convinced him that Christian morality was repressive and undermined the full moral autonomy of the individual. To Nietzsche there was nothing of greater importance than human freedom, not simply in the sense of being able to choose between alternative actions, but in the larger sense of being freed from any moral constraints whatsoever. Nietzsche would develop this fundamental intuition with a vengeance throughout his life.

While at university he read many of the radical left-wing Hegelians and decided as a result to abandon his Christian upbringing. By all accounts Nietzsche was one of the greatest minds of Western intellectual history and undoubtedly one of Christianity's sharpest critics ever. It is significant that the university of Leipzig granted him a full academic doctorate without his having fulfilled any of the core requirements, least of all a doctoral dissertation. More amazing still, Nietzsche was promoted to being a full professor in philology the year after being given his academic doctorate, having never taught a class nor written a book. In this light it makes sense why Nietzsche prized intellectual genius and saw it as a flowering of the ancient virtue of creativity in a similar ilk to the great musicians and poets. He came to view Christianity as a repression of this creativity and thereby civilization's worst enemy.

His analysis was not cool and dispassionate like many of the earlier post-Enlightenment thinkers. There was no pretence of an objective sifting of the evidence for and against religion. 'Disinteredness has no value either in heaven or on earth.'[15] Nietzsche understood that reason could never be objective. Reason, a tool in the service of desire, could clarify only the stark choices facing all humans. The first and most important choice concerned God. Nietzsche believed with all

---

[15] Nietzsche 1974: 128.

his heart that if there was a God, Nietzsche could not be free. If he were free, there could be no God. It was that simple – and yet that terrifying. If this was the beginning of the story, it was also the end. To get from start to finish it is important to follow Nietzsche's path along the way.

In his most notable work, *Thus Spake Zarathustra*, Nietzsche painted a picture of two competing world views. He referred to one as the logic of life and the other as the logic of reason. In the former, human existence was the most primal datum. All else came from this. It accepted life simply as it was: to be celebrated and enjoyed. The logic of reason on the other hand imposed a framework of meaning around life in such a manner that human existence was interpreted through a moral and religious framework. Nietzsche represented these conflicting world views by appeal to the ancient mythological figures of Dionysius and Apollos. Dionysius was the god of wine and song. He celebrated life in all its pleasures and all its dangers. Apollos by contrast was the god of order and balance. For Apollos life was not so much to be celebrated as to be organized and interpreted. Beauty was the celebration of harmony and symmetry for Apollos. For Dionysius there was no such thing as beauty except that which came from the flowering of creative genius. Beauty was enjoyed when life was lived to the fullest for Dionysius. By contrast Apollos preached, 'Know thyself and do nothing in excess.' Dionysius proclaimed, 'Celebrate the excess of life always.'

Whom should we choose, Dionysius or Apollos? According to Nietzsche this was the fundamental choice between the logic of life and the logic of reason. It was also a choice that could not be settled by appeal to reasons – for that would already assume the conclusion the evidence was intended to support. The choice was absolute and absolutely arbitrary. Life could not be chosen *because* it was 'right', for this would be to choose the logic of reason. There can be no reasons in favour of reason, nor in favour of life.

Nietzsche had in effect claimed that all morality and truth in the end were arbitrary – for every argument must start initially with premises that cannot be supported. The original foundation of every argument is merely 'suspended in air'. First principles are simply and only arbitrary choices, if they are indeed the principles upon which all other principles stand. In this regard first principles cannot be reasonable or rational if they are indeed *first principles*, for there would be no principles prior to first principles by which to judge whether the first principles satisfied them as reasonable.

If we think of foundationalism as that system of logic committed to rational first principles, Nietzsche heralded the end of foundationalism. At the time most thought of foundationalism as the logical framework of Christian belief. Christians believed in first principles as laid out in Holy Scripture. Few realized that the Enlightenment critiques of Christian belief were every bit as foundational in structure. 'Trust only empirical evidence' may seem like a reasonable first principle – but on what basis is it reasonable? None, unless one also *assumes* that empirical evidence only is reasonable.

The upshot was that rationality came to be seen by Nietzsche as a function of human choice. Rationality was located in human subjectivity rather than any objective rational order. What this entailed was that humans created their own meaning, the logic that made sense of their own lives. They could cede that responsibility to others, but in doing so would themselves have chosen to be slaves to another's authority over them. Religious people were the worst culprits in this regard. They consigned themselves to the absolute definition by another, and thereby lost altogether what it was that made them truly human: the awful responsibility to choose for oneself.

Nietzsche referred to this 'awful responsibility' as the will to power. It was the assertion of the self as the source of meaning. It was the intuition that humans created rather than discovered the world in which their meaning was fixed. In this humans did not find so much as make truth. In contrast to Christianity as well as to the history of the Western philosophical tradition, Nietzsche believed humans did not have a fixed nature. They bore the burden of having to create meaning out of nothing. The Christian tradition had given the illusion that God bore that burden, but, in so doing, Christians had abandoned their true humanity. 'We should not place perfection above in the heavens or in a place of time nor should we set ourselves a perfection which is unattainable. Man is what man can make of himself.'[16]

If the will to power was the essence of what it meant to be human, then there could be no being who exercised the will to power over another. Most especially, Nietzsche argued, if humans were to exercise their will to power, then God could not be. He had to die if man was to live. For this reason Nietzsche declared God was dead. And if dead, then humankind had to face up to their plight. There was no ultimate meaning to life – only the meaning individuals could create for themselves. There was no absolute good and evil either. The only good left

---

[16] Nietzsche 1987: 32.

was that which enhanced the feeling of power in each individual to determine his or her own destiny.

Nietzsche believed that in the absence of God and meaning, individuals had to assert a dialectical courage. This was a courage to face up to the consequences of meaninglessness, no longer holding onto the illusion that real absolute meaning could be found or created. This was a call to courage when one knew ultimately that courage would not save. This was the courage to live meaninglessly. Nietzsche understood that few could ever fully face this reality. The person who could overcome the hopelessness of the human plight by the sheer force of his or her will to power Nietzsche called an *Übermensch* (superperson). In this he was profoundly influenced by the tragic heroes of ancient Greek mythology who fought the gods rather than merely accept their fate.

With the foundation of theism destroyed, and nothing but the will to power left, Nietzsche believed Judeo-Christian morality would eventually crumble. If God were dead, the moral constructs of good and evil would vanish. There would be no room for guilt if right and wrong no longer existed. The only good left would be those actions that were life affirming. All of traditional morality was turned upside down, what Nietzsche called the 'transvaluation of all values'. Whereas traditional morality valued love of God and love of neighbour, abhorring love of self, Nietzsche believed the only value left would be love of self. Christianity had celebrated humility and meekness, obedience and loyalty. These were moral values for slaves and the weak. The courage to face up to the meaninglessness of life on one's own terms demanded a morality for self-determining masters.

Nietzsche believed that the rejection of traditional morality was in part accomplished by locating the genesis of moral development, what he called a 'genealogy of morals'. By locating morality within the story of the past, the pretense to an eternal and transcendent beginning could be abolished. The story of the two moralities (slave and master) arose in cultures that denied desire and endorsed the weaknesses of the masses. The slave morality developed out of fear and hatred of the master class. The impotent, unable to conquer their more worthy and physically powerful foes, sought 'spiritual revenge'. They made everything that was opposed to the master class 'good'. Aligning God with their cause, they endorsed the eternal damnation of everyone who violated their moral standards. Eternal damnation was the ultimate revenge, and by it Nietzsche claimed to show that Judeo-Christian morality was rooted not in love but in hatred and vengefulness.

He believed this genealogy of morals was itself sufficient to undermine the slave morality of Christianity by manifesting the stark differences between the two moralities. Christianity was for weak people. Atheism demanded a passionate embrace of strength. Christianity sought to sublimate the core instincts and desires of humanity. Atheism declared that primal instincts and desires should be affirmed. Christianity imposed order by introducing absolutes. Atheism celebrated the chaos of life. Christianity defended the slave morality. Atheism rejected the slave morality and rejoiced that everyone was their own master.

The choice between these alternative moralities and world views was clear and unavoidable, and Christians ought to thank Nietzsche for that clarity. More than anyone else, he was willing to face the consequences of atheism. Liberal Christianity had tried to domesticate religion, making it appear more 'civilized', but had denuded it in the process while also trying to avoid the spiritual and moral consequences of its naturalism. The earlier secular prophets had got rid of God, but supposed there was ample room for meaningful existence without him, based largely on the optimistic assumption of human goodness. Nietzsche saw more starkly than his predecessors that without God there was no goodness left, either in humankind or anywhere else. Nietzsche put to rest any easy atheism, as much as the earlier secular prophets had put to death easy believism. Believing in God had no room for making him in one's own image. By a mirror reasoning Nietzsche believed that atheism had no room for naive hope and optimism. Without God, life was meaningless.

Nietzsche lived the courage of his convictions. He left academic life, believing that it survived by creating an artificial cocoon of ideas. He served for a time in the ambulance corps in the Franco-Prussian war of 1870–71, in some measure because of his own ill health. During the decade of the 1880s, while suffering from deep clinical depression and wandering around Europe, he wrote his most penetrating and cryptic works. At the end of the decade severe mental illness set in, probably due to a venereal disease acquired during many earlier promiscuous sexual encounters. For the last decade of his life he lived in the care of his mother and sister. It is a strange irony that Nietzsche died while hallucinating that he was Jesus Christ, his greatest enemy.

Chapter Eight

Significance and security in a new key

Relationships are the key to happiness. People who live in
the densest social networks tend to flourish, while people
who live with few social bonds are much more prone to
depression and suicide.

(Brooks 2008: A21)

The canonical relationship between imaging and idolatry suggests
that the *imago Dei* is fundamentally a relational term but one with a
peculiar relationship in view. It draws attention to the way in which
the image reflects the original as its primary relation. The image is
conceptually like a shadow, ontologically dependent upon the object
it reflects. It is the imaging relationship rather than the image itself
that is the primary vantage point throughout Scripture. It is perfectly
appropriate to talk about the image as an object in its own right, but
it is conceptually impoverished if this is the primary discourse we
use to think about the image. The two fundamental claims from the
biblical-theological argument of the previous chapters can be stated
simply. The inextricably relational character of imaging language
across the canon forces us to affirm both the social character of human
identity as well as its fundamentally liturgical nature in relationship
to God.

It is also appropriate to say, Christianly speaking, that a relationship
to God is that which secures our identity as humans. Our existing as
people is rooted in our relation to God. It is also true to say, asymmetrically, that God's existence is not rooted in a relation to humanity.
It is rooted in the triune relationships that exist prior to and apart
from creation.[1] And further that the very permanence of God is that
which grounds the independence of the triune persons from human

---

[1] It is not my central concern to enter into the theological discussion of the Trinity,
which is quite naturally where these themes would need much greater elaboration.

personhood. It is the very transitory character of human personhood that manifests a dependence in the triune persons. It is the nature of that 'transitoriness' and thereby 'dependence' that the Scriptures depict with the language of 'image'.

The divine community (Trinity) is the blueprint of the redeemed ecclesial community, and the *Godness* of God is what secures the ecclesial community as a redeemed image and by which the original and the image are distinguished. It is God by virtue of his being God who grants significance to the human community and who also redeems or reconciles that community. It is the ontological 'weight' of God that serves as the foundational assumption in the redemptive-historical account of humans as created, redeemed or consummated images. It is not just any sociality that defines the human person but a sociality whose *telos* is found in the permanence of God – in his very *Godness*.[2]

The very 'ordinariness' of biblical language supposes that God's *oneness* is not a theological abstraction from his *threeness*.[3] Nor is God's *threeness* a theological abstraction from his oneness. The substantiality of divine unity ought not to undermine the sociality of the divine Trinity. But neither should the sociality of the divine Trinity undermine the substantiality of the divine unity. If evangelical theology has insufficiently appreciated the sociality of the divine Trinity, it has nonetheless recognized the substantiality of the divine unity. In ordinary language this means that there is only one God who is worthy of worship.

Human identity is wrapped up in the dialectical relationship of the community to its constitutive elements – people.[4] As social creatures we do not exist independently of society, and theologically we do not exist apart from the reflecting relation to the divine community.

---

[2] To use other words, the economic Trinity and the immanent Trinity are both theologically significant grounds of a fuller conception of the *imago Dei*. It is the ontological weight of the immanent Trinity that underlies the relational significance of the economic Trinity for a doctrine of human personhood. This would suggest that collapsing of the immanent Trinity into the economic Trinity in Rahner (and Barth) is flawed. The consensus of the church prior to the twentieth century would also suggest this.

[3] Deut. 6:4: 'The LORD our God, the LORD is one.' The prophet Malachi asks rhetorically, 'Has not one God created us?' (Mal. 2:10). The epistle of Romans affirms, 'since God is one – who will justify the circumcised by faith and the uncircumcised through faith' (Rom. 3:30).

[4] This is Berger's point when he writes, 'It is within society, and as a result of social processes, that the individual becomes a person, that he attains and holds onto an identity, and that he carries out the various projects that constitute his life. The person cannot exist apart from society' (Berger 1967: 3).

Human significance rests precisely in what or whom humans reflect and the relationships in which those reflections occur.

Individual people are never people outside a web of relationships. Identity is given by virtue of the intrinsically relational character of personhood. This means that the search for personal identity is a function of the web of relationships in which each individual is engaged. People take their clues as to who they are from the other people who speak into their lives. The individual's own voice undoubtedly is part of this 'identity-forming conversation', but it is only one voice among others. The 'identity-forming conversation' is not mechanical in its working, nor is it predictable in any recognizable way. The biblical-theological claim also runs against the grain of the modern intuition that personal identity refers to an essence deep in a person's psyche – what the Cartesian tradition might have referred to as the 'self'. Late modernity has produced a heightened interest in the 'self' but it has been an interest without due regard for the ultimate purpose of the self – honouring or delighting in the living God.[5]

The biblical account also runs against the grain of the contemporary intuition that personal identity is identifiable with the peculiar character traits of ethnicity, race, sexual orientation or gender. The web of relationships described in the Scriptures is far richer and more complex than any one of these could encompass. Even more importantly none of these characteristics captures the essential divine–human relationship at the heart of an accurate description of personal identity.

The sociality of the human person is never a sociality *simpliciter*. It is never merely a set of human relationships by itself. Relationships always manifest and point to a liturgical impulse in the *imago Dei*, where the *imago Dei* is constituted by a yearning for satisfaction or fulfilment in that reflecting relation. The intrinsic desire for fulfilment is hardwired into the sociality of the human person. It is precisely this yearning for completion that draws humans into relationships, and makes those relationships fragile and open to corruption. Though God could have chosen to create differently, he in fact did create humans in his image who are completed and fulfilled in their relationship to him.

---

[5] Cf. Craig Gay (1998) for helpful insights into the character of modernity as a technological kind of institution that reshapes human desire in its own image. Gay's final chapter, 'Toward a Theology of Personhood', suggests the danger of idolatry in the context of the modern world though he underscores the tendency towards reductionism whenever idolatry is highlighted as theologically significant.

The human–divine relationship is reflected and refracted in the way in which humans relate to one another. Elements of human–human relationships grant significance and security to people in partial as well as pleasant and/or painful ways. The varying nature of relationships runs the spectrum from intimate to hostile – and often the same relationship can swing to both ends of that spectrum across time. Some relationships bear marks of intimacy and hostility at the same time. Marriage and sibling relationships are of this sort. Familial relationships are different from other kinds of relationships (business partners, teammates, co-workers, etc.) in that the relationship is its own end, sustained (or not) without reference to an external functional end. Familial relationships are a species of friendships, to be valued because of the intrinsic character of the relationship rather than as a means to another end.

Marriage is a unique form of friendship, valued not only because of the intimacy of the relationship, but also because of its enduring nature. It is not an accident that marriage is the primary illustration of the human–divine relationship across the Scriptures. Marriage is instituted to protect the significance of each spouse, even as it also finds its security in the safety it is intended to provide. Marriage is also the most painful relationship when it goes awry. There is no pain like the emotional agony experienced in a broken marriage.

Relationships of intimacy sustain us, and broken relationships undermine our sense of significance. This is the natural result of the way in which God has made us. The deeper point throughout the Scriptures is that this hardwiring relational character of humankind is a reflection of God's relational character and the relationally perfect love one member of the Trinity has towards the other members.

When the intimacy of the divine–human relationship is broken, significance and security are shattered as well. The fracturing of the relationship inevitably creates a yearning for something else to provide significance and security. Though there is not anyone or anything that can provide that ultimate significance and security except for the triune God, individuals will search for a substitute. This is the initial dynamic of idolatry.

At the heart of worship is a sense of 'giving yourself away' to another. Key to worship then are the questions 'To whom are you are giving yourself away and in what manner are you giving yourself?' Genuine worship is giving yourself to the living God in whom and for whom you have been created. Idolatry by contrast is substituting the true object of worship (God) for an imitation (idol) and reorienting the relationship from worship to possession. One who worships the living God does not possess him for one's own purposes.[6] But those who create an idol seek to possess it for their own purpose. Martin Buber supposed that idols turn people into objects – and therefore even God could be worshipped idolatrously, that is as an object for human purposes.[7] This is the difference between the image of reflection and the idols of possession.[8]

An idol is desired as a means to an end, and the end is significance and security on the individual's own terms. But a strange reality sets in with idols. Since significance and security cannot be fulfilled by the idol, the idol creates a deeper longing for significance and security for that which it cannot provide. This results in a chasing after the idol, driven by the conviction that eventually the idol will somehow provide the promised significance and security. The cycle repeats itself. Longing provides the opportunity to chase, and chasing creates a deeper longing. Effectively the idol possesses the one who fashioned it. The yearning for significance and security that initiated the dynamic of idolatry has in fact led to a deeper dissatisfaction and a greater frustration – a dissatisfaction and frustration caused by inability of the idol to fulfil that which it appeared to promise.

The worshipping relationship to the triune God restrains the idolatrous intentions of possession and consumption, and as it restrains them it causes the worshipper to become an alien of a sort in the wider culture of consumption. And if the unleashing of desire for consumptive purposes is near the centre of our present cultural story, those who worship the living God must feel a certain unease with the

---

[6] It is intriguing that the secular prophets of the nineteenth century (Ludwig Feuerbach, Karl Marx, Friedrich Nietzsche, etc.) levelled the charge of idolatry against Christianity itself, supposing that the God of Christianity had been created in the church's own image as a means to further its own interests. An intended trajectory of Westphal 1994 is the comparison of the Old Testament prophet's use of the language of idolatry and the secular prophet's usage of the same.

[7] Buber (1970: 110) writes, 'Whoever has been converted by substitution, now "has" a phantom that he calls God. God, however, the eternal presence, cannot be had. Woe unto the possessed who fancy they possess God.'

[8] A lengthy secondary literature arose from Goffman's (1959) sociological study, owing in some measure to Goffman's provocative insight that human identity in the modern era was accompanied by the pressure to manage an image. 'Image management' became an increasingly fruitful construct to speak about the postmodern extension of the modern turn to the subject. It is not difficult to coordinate the preceding canonical account of the *imago Dei* to Goffman's insights about the 'art of impression management'. The best analysis of Goffman's legacy can be found in Tseelon 1992: 115–128.

core values of our times.[9] They must recognize the peculiar idolatries of possession that arise in an era of affluence and consumption.[10] Idolatries of possession are peculiarly strong in eras of affluence when the plethora of material possessions gives the illusion of spiritual progress and prosperity, thereby masking the addictions of materialism and consumerism.

The crisis of identity and the idolatries of consumption

The crisis many people experience in daily life is one of significance and safety. It is not an abstract crisis but has the larger questions of purpose and meaning in view. The central battle zone of the crisis may be one's job or marriage or reputation, though the sense of crisis has to do with how these realities are connected to the wider meaning of one's life. In a world in which time appears to move very rapidly for ordinary people the disjunction between the number of 'things' on one's schedule and the significance of the schedule as a whole is often acute. Our lives move at such a pace we can barely remember what is actually important any longer. There is often too much busyness to sense anything meaningful in life. Many of us are too busy to slow down long enough to find life satisfying. If our lives are a story, the story seems to have too much filler and too little real plot. We sense our lives would not make a good novel. There are too many parts to ordinary life to keep it coherent in any recognizable sense, and it is too complicated to untangle or savour.

As life becomes more complicated it becomes more ambiguous. It becomes more difficult to find a set of focal concerns that give meaning and sustain life.[11] As a result life also becomes more shallow. It begins to feel plastic.[12] Ordinary life reads like a plastic

---

[9] From a different angle Clapp (1997) captures this central cultural impulse in evangelical perspective.

[10] Our present cultural context may aptly be referred to as *modernity*. Its central characteristics are industrial processes, technological innovations, urbanization and consumer capitalism. By contrast the term *modernism* refers to the ideologies that accompanied the rise of these cultural structures, and whose central figures are associated with the eighteenth-century movement known as the Enlightenment.

[11] Borgmann 2003.

[12] I recall one of the opening lines in the classic film of the 1960s *The Graduate*, when a neighbour tells the young directionless college student (played by Dustin Hoffman) that 'the future is plastic'. This was an era-defining statement about the shallowness of modern life embedded in the pervasive and technologically inspired affluence of the post-war economic boom.

SIGNIFICANCE AND SECURITY

narrative.[13] It is surrounded by artificial constructs in films, television and Internet entertainment made to imitate the real world but at critical junctures deviating from reality in order to achieve a set of higher purposes, namely to enact a consumer economic transaction. These artificial constructs reshape the human heart, which in turn imagines it can live in this pseudo-paradise with the eschatological hope that there will eventually be enough money to make it come true. The words of its central refrain, 'If you can pay for it, you can do it,' appear almost as a covenantal promise. Part of the very enchantment of these plastic narratives is that they appear inter-woven with the delights of our own desires. As a cultural critic once wrote of Disney World, 'They can be forgiven a certain amount of hubris because the laws of reality do not operate there.'[14] Likewise our plastic narratives create a set of unrealistic expectations that promise fulfilment. The consumer-driven narrative is a story where the streets are always clean, where everyone has a smile on their face and where the triumph of human creativity reaches apparent perfection – Disneyesque in its proportions.

It is also a story that would prefer to postpone the truth question. The important uncertainty is not whether the story matches up with reality, but rather whether the story is enjoyable. The last half century of rising affluence came with an internal logic of faith in progress and happiness, even as a more cynical mood settled into North American life as a result of vast inequities of affluence. The ironic pairing of these two contrasting moods (happiness and cynicism) left little room for transcendent realities. Life in a consumer culture was lived without external reference points. It was a story with its own language, thought-forms and practices within which consumers searched for the fulfilment of desires.[15] Marketing had become a quintessential task in late modernity as the means to ensure that truth was irrelevant and self-definition all important. Whatever notion of truth remained appeared as a mere relationship between a set of products to be sold and a set of desires that would pay a price for satisfaction. It is a story which tells us that our desires are worth satisfying and yet implicitly tells us which desires are more important than others, and then commodifies those desires. The gratification of those desires comes primarily with an economic purchase.

[13] I (2000: 91–110) have earlier referred to this phenomenon as a 'vinyl narrative'.
[14] Fjellman 1992: 204.
[15] To use Lindbeck's (1984) categories, it was a cultural-linguistic system of the very profoundest sort.

It is a world created for us, which in turn recreates us in its image.[16] We have become consumers because we live in a consumer culture. No one is at fault here. We are all at fault. We buy the image because we want it and it is the raw desire for happiness that drives most transactions in these plastic narratives. As Woody Allen once claimed in his sordid trial defending his affair with his adopted step-daughter, 'the heart wants what it wants'.[17] We are so enchanted by the plastic world of our idols that we believe the heart gets what it wants.

While all of the consumer structures of culture take shape around us, we too often naively suppose the world has changed but we have remained relatively unchanged. The world may be filled with techno-logical innovations undreamt of fifty years ago – cyberspace devices, social media networks and advanced medical technologies – but the reality is that the greater change has occurred in how we relate to our world, what we think about ourselves and, last but not least, the ways in which religious faith has been transformed.

One of the striking facts of late modernity is the way in which these technologies have reordered our inner consciousness. The gadgets of our age have exerted enormous pressure to reshape the categories of our mental life. We think differently about the world we live in because of the world we live in. We believe the plastic narratives because after all 'the heart wants what it wants'.

One of the fundamental changes in modern consciousness is the movement from fate to choice.[18] The power of our tools creates so many more choices than could have been conceived by any earlier civilization. The vast array of things possible now through our technological innov-ations makes it appear that an individual has unlimited power and unlimited choices. We are not bound by the fates of history any longer.

But the choices created by our tools represent only a small slice of an enormously larger array of choices that are part of the taken-for-granted fabric of life in the first part of the third millennium AD: choices of occupation, of place of residence, of marriage, of the number of one's children, of one's holiday destination. The list goes on with regard to the external arrangements of life. But there are other choices, inner choices, that deeply touch the consciousness of individuals: lifestyle choices, religious choices and moral choices.[19]

---

[16] Berger 1967.

[17] Elshtain 1993: 12.

[18] This argument is laid out most clearly in Berger 1979.

[19] The abortion debate is cast in these terms, as is the contemporary controversy over sexual preferences. Choice becomes the operative mental category in modern life.

The more choices, the more reflection. The individual who reflects becomes more conscious of himself. He turns his attention from the objectively given outside world to his own subjectivity. As he does this, two things happen simultaneously: the outside world becomes more questionable and his own inner world becomes more complex. People become more suspicious of any solution that appears as the 'only' one. The hegemony of truth itself comes under severe scrutiny.

And ironically, the greater amount of reflection on our own inner subjectivity results in far less reflection about 'ultimate matters'. Steven Fjellman has written:

> The world of commodities presents itself in an onslaught of discrete, disconnected packages, and the pursuit of these packages – each designed to fill some artificially constructed need – leaves minimal space in our lives for coherent critical thought about what we are doing. We are encouraged to pay attention only to those things that are amusing and fun.[20]

It is this critical dynamic of human identity that is at the heart of the biblical argument against idols. The plastic narratives of our times suggests that reality is eminently mouldable into our image, that our image and identity are profoundly flexible and ought to be shaped according to our deepest desires, and finally that those desires are most fruitful when empowered with choice. This is the mega-narrative of late modernity.

Christian identity and plastic narratives

The challenge for all of us is the influence of this plastic story upon our apprehension of the biblical narrative of the *imago Dei*. Religious activity where it exists in this world has increasingly been com-partmentalized into a private experience.[21] Religion is privately meaningful and publicly irrelevant.[22] Religious faith has increasingly ceased to be the glue that holds the world together for boomers, busters and millennials. It is simply one piece of a very large puzzle, and is simply one narrative among many. The modern religious narrative appears as plastic in our public discourse precisely because

[20] Fjellman 1992: 247.
[21] On this note see Nash 1994 and the perceptive analysis of evangelicals in the business community.
[22] Berger 1967: 133.

every story is construed as artificially constructed. There is no cultural space for an integrating story of the rest of reality, nor a mega-narrative originating in a transcendent source. Every story is one story among others, simply narrating a distinctive compartment of our imagination and desires.

One of the greatest obstacles to recovering an identity rooted in the gospel is the plastic-like designation conferred on all the narratives in our times – including the gospel narrative.[23] Christians run an enormous risk if they interpret their identity as simply an arbitrarily chosen one among the myriad of possible ones. If our *raison d'être* emerges from the plastic narratives of our times, we will be endlessly tossed to and fro by the winds of our own dissatisfactions. But it is by honestly facing the dissatisfaction with our idols that an opportunity arises to restore a more genuine and authentic identity.

The cultural captivity of evangelicalism is by now a well-chronicled story. The consumer character of modern church life is a subject upon which there has already developed a healthy consensus and scepticism. Robert Wuthnow has argued eloquently that in their more candid moments evangelicals admit to being thoroughly materialistic (while deploring this trait in their children). They believe in the proverbial bottom line. They shoulder greater and greater personal economic obligations and fret about how to pay their bills. These are matters of sheer necessity, they tell themselves. But they also enlist hearts and minds. Gainful employment supplies us with a purpose for living. But in our modern context work has become a means of self-expression and no less so for evangelicals than non-evangelicals. Careers have replaced callings both inside and outside the church. Having money is too often the secret key to happiness. Correspondingly, financial setbacks destroy self-esteem. We associate freedom with having the latest iPhone, a townhouse in the city, an Audi A6 or whatever the latest symbols of material wealth may be.

---

[23] This has not happened because there was some grand intellectual conspiracy in the last century or our own that determined for ever the course of the gospel's identity. No, rather the confluence of very complex factors, some ideological and some not very ideological at all, created the context in which it seemed only 'natural' that all narratives should in the end prove to be no more than arbitrary and self-determining. The historical and philosophical precedents to this transforming narrative have been told elsewhere. Let me suggest Rorty's (1981) sympathetic treatment of these matters. Believing that Nietzsche was the patriarch of this conceptual framework, one could also fruitfully peruse Westphal (1994) for the same story. Michael Horton (2002) tells the story in great detail and very much in sympathy with the line of argument I am following.

Compare the weekly sermon seventy-five million Americans hear each Sunday morning with the daily bombardment of television commercials to which they are exposed, or the 'do this or get fired' pressures they experience at work. Put a few thousand dollars in their pocket and send a young couple out to make a down payment on a new car: how much is some vague religious teaching about stewardship going to matter, compared with arguments about sportiness and acceleration?

Christian faith is, as a result, an ambiguous presence in the evangelical churchgoing population. It sends mixed signals about work, telling them to work hard but not too hard. It counsels us to be diligent with our money but seldom instructs us how to be diligent. Indeed it raises our anxieties about money and discourages us from talking openly about them. It warns us against the excessive materialism that pervades our society but offers little to keep us from the temptations of materialism. Feeling ambivalent about the role of wealth, evangelicals therefore go about their lives pretty much the same as those who have no faith at all.

The populist character of the evangelical movement has given it an enduring relevance in a deeply populist culture, such as America has been across the last two centuries. It has also made it susceptible to the plastic-like character of the contemporary contexts. The theological vision of the evangelical movement has been created in large measure by popularizers and celebrity pastors, individuals with no other perceivable gift than the ability to communicate effectively. It is given legitimization by popular vote, usually in the form of large conferences organized by the modern 'circuit riders'. And it survives by the creation of simple slogans and mediums of communication void of serious reflection. These communication techniques work on the assumption that the world out there is straightforward and void of ambiguity.

Likewise the Bible is studied primarily with the aid of all-too-simplistic Bible study materials. The fundamental question asked of the text is 'What does it say to me?'[24] Implicit is an assumption about the essential clarity of the text and its accessibility to any person who would briefly consider it. The practice of the small-group Bible studies does encourage individuals to read the Bible as they have never done before, but encourages them to read the text according to their

[24] I am indebted to a former colleague, T. David Gordon, for the following line of argument. This is most clearly spelled out in his unpublished paper 'The Hidden Assumptions of Small Group Bible Study'.

own subjective interests.[25] The Bible becomes captive to the whims of individuals and therefore continues to sit too lightly on their lives. The irony is that our celebrity pastors serve as papal-like interpreters of the Bible in public settings, and individuals are trained to read the Bible as if no one has read the Bible before them. The interplay between these two factors reinforces a pattern wherein the Bible is subject to multiple opinions. Its authoritative force is diminished. By avoiding the aid of the community of interpreters across the history of the church and around the globe there has been a reinforcement of the power of the biases of our own individual situation. The Scriptures become refashioned in our own image, becoming an object we possess rather than our being possessed by them.

Along with most other Christian traditions in our day the evangelical movement is largely post-denominational. The direct effect of this is that individuals do not inhabit a theological tradition but reside in a nebulous heritage, a heritage with little substance and no sharp edges. It is an ecclesiology rooted not in concrete traditions, but in the ambiguity of style and taste. It is not a commitment that has much to say about soteriology or the sacraments, about church and culture or about biblical theology. It is a heritage that cannot speak to all of life, because its concerns are driven by relevance to modern life.

Evangelical worship may well serve to communicate the gospel in a medium intelligible to many contemporary citizens of our culture, but it often does so without recognizing the unintended consequences of its own ordinary language. The rhetoric of evangelical piety reinforces the 'story-like' character of the Christian life – but a story rooted in the constructs of our time. It is an artificial medium whose primary intent is to fulfil the desire for happiness. Its hidden assumption is that the world unfolds before our eyes on the terms of ordinary modern life.

The evangelical tradition has too frequently embraced the 'solitary minds' of modernity as the means to resist the tyranny of corrupting communities. And in doing so has left itself open to the danger of reflecting the idolatries of our peculiar age of consumption. The evangelical sense of sociality rests too lightly on its understanding of the Christian faith, and the privileging of the individual has weighed too heavily in its soteriology. The 'Christian life' has too little space for the 'Christian community'. Often lost in practice is the sense of being covenantly bound to the people of God as a reflection of the triune

---

[25] This same point is argued for briefly in Johnson 1990: 17–22.

God to whom that individual is also covenantly bound. From this perspective it looks like evangelicals have not resisted the plastic narratives of the age.

A contrasting word must be spoken to this common 'cultural captivity' narrative of evangelicals. The evangelical tradition has resisted central cultural pressures with its emphasis upon the uniqueness of the gospel – a uniqueness grounded in the claim that there is only one God. The God revealed is the one divine being who requires an experiential encounter, who enacts the grounds of the encounter and who authorizes the narrating of that encounter on the pages of Scripture. All of this points inextricably to Jesus Christ. It is Jesus Christ in whom the experiential encounter takes place. It is Jesus Christ who enacts that encounter in his incarnation. And it is the narrative of Jesus Christ as the Alpha and Omega of the canon of Scripture that is the hermeneutical centre of the gospel. In each of these ways the uniqueness of Jesus Christ is the necessary ground for the resistance of idolatry, the very idolatry to which evangelicals are in other ways so susceptible. But it is this resource that is integral to the evangelical tradition (and the 'Great Tradition' of Christianity) that is the ground for the hope of exodus from its present cultural captivity and is a route through which personhood might be recovered as a 'being-in-relation' reflecting and honouring the 'Three-in-One' living God.

An eternal story told across time

Let me turn my attention finally to a consideration of the unique opportunities in our highly partisan world of plastic narratives to recover the biblical narrative of the *imago Dei*. Those opportunities are connected to the reawakening of the power of stories in our culture. The Christian's hope is bound up with the story of God's redemption in history, which gives meaning to the past, explains the present and provides guidance for the future. If our identity seems rooted too often in our yearning for yet greater and better comforts and conveniences promised by our consumer culture, then the unmasking of those objects as idols in an unsatisfying narrative may point the way forward. The narrative of Scripture is not simply a story of ancient events; it is a story that continues to interpret the idols of every age through its lens. It interprets our present identity by giving a different set of glasses through which we see ourselves and our world. These glasses give us a new 'way of looking at the world' that is distinctively theological in character. It is distinctively theological in the sense that it connects everything to the reality that we are creatures in the image of the living God and made to find our security and significance in all that he is.[26]

We have also come to recognize that stories require a community to provide them with a living plausibility. As social creatures, communities are required to provide legitimacy to a 'way of looking at the world'. Ecclesial communities in particular will either reinforce a theological way of seeing reality, providing it with 'oomph',[27] or they will adopt and adapt to the plurality of narratives that swirl around them. The living community of faith is that community commissioned to bring to life the story of eternity so to speak.

This simply is to claim that the church is the context for our identity, but in a time when the church sits lightly on the minds and hearts of many Christians in the West it is not a surprise that Christian identity has become so fragile.[28] What is it that holds our identity together in and through the church? The presence of the risen Lord in the preaching of the Word and the celebration of the sacraments through which the Spirit has so chosen to make this presence manifest. This presence is intimately rooted in the history of redemption and it is that story which the church continually rehearses in its worship. It is the story of the church that is the larger story of any individual Christian.

It is the story of God's redemptive presence that connects the past, present and future and thereby connects us with the living God.[29] At the beginning God spoke creation into being. His presence throughout creation is everywhere assumed and yet he remains distinctly separate from his creation. God created by the power of his Word and gave life and breath to his creatures by his Spirit. In this, as at all other critical junctures of redemptive history, there is a manifest presence of the triune God, Father Son and Spirit.

It is imperative to understand that God's presence is an ordered presence at the beginning. It is a presence whose boundaries he himself has set. He determines the nature and purpose of creation and the manner in which it will reflect him. The two cultural mandates, to be fruitful and multiply and to be stewards of the garden, are reflections

---

[26] Elsewhere I (1993) have referred to this simply as a theological vision.

[27] 'Oomph' is a technical term common among linguistically challenged theologians.

[28] Bolsinger 2004.

[29] It is that connectedness of time that evangelicalism so desperately needs. Evangelicals live fragmented lives because they have cut themselves off from time and the one who created it.

of the character of God himself. It is also God who determines the relationship between his creatures and himself. He is the one who defines good and evil and is the one who placed Adam on probation in his presence.

In Genesis 3, when sin is introduced, God's presence becomes a threat to the existence of Adam and Eve and the serpent. It is a threatening presence. As a result the original couple are removed from the immediate presence of God, cast out of the garden. The flaming swords guarding the garden are the reminders that Adam and Eve will not return to God's immediate presence except through judgment. Cain is further punished for his sin by for ever losing a home, ever to be a pilgrim on a journey.

With the renewed presence of God to Abraham in Genesis 12 there is a recovery of the fellowship of the garden, yet deepened in ways unforeseen earlier. God promises to be with Abraham, to make of him a great nation and to give him a land flowing with milk and honey. God promises a presence, a people and a place. In all of this he renames Abram, reminding him that it is ultimately God who redemptively establishes purpose and identity. God's words are accompanied by his promises to be fulfilled in actions. Word and deed go hand in hand.

We reach another redemptive climax in the call of Moses. God shows himself present to Moses in the burning bush. During Moses' entire life God manifested himself in unique miracles – showing himself not only to be the Lord of nature, but also the Lord who will use nature for the redemption of his creatures. The Red Sea is parted and the people baptized into Moses, as the one who will take them to the Promised Land. But in God's providence Moses does not take them into the Promised Land. He looks at Canaan from the other side of the Jordan, foreshadowing the future Redeemer who will take God's people into the Promised Land of God's presence eternally. At Sinai Moses is given a glimpse of God's direct presence but only of his back. God determines that Israel will hear him when they listen to Moses. A tent of meeting was constructed where God would be present to Moses and over which the pillar of cloud would rest, signifying God's abiding presence.

When the people were finally taken into the Promised Land, it was not until David's rule that the land was entirely brought under Israelite rule. As Moses was not permitted to enter the Promised Land, so David was not permitted to build the temple where God's name would rest. That task was left to the son of David, Solomon. Then at the temple God's redemption was graphically acted out in the sacrificial cultus. The people were reminded that the presence of God was still largely protected – the Holy of Holies was entered into only once a year and then only by the high priest. God's presence was mediated and severely restricted.

The climax of God's redemptive promise occurred with the coming of God himself in the flesh. The apostle John tells us that in Christ God has come to tabernacle in our midst. The fullness of God dwells in Christ, and in our union with Christ in his death and resurrection we are given new life – the breadth of God's Spirit. The veil of Moses is lifted from our faces when we come to Christ and now we see God face to face – in Christ. Christ is both God and also the mediator of God's presence for his people.

The life and breadth of the Spirit are given in and through the body of our Lord – in his death and resurrection. It is extended to us spiritually in the calling of the church, in its proclamation of the gospel and its practice of the sacraments as the tangible signs of the gospel. Though we still 'see' God through a glass darkly, we wait expectantly for that day when his presence will no longer be mediated for us.

We await the day when God himself will reside in the midst of his people. On that day he will wipe away all our tears and no longer will there be a sun or moon, for the Lord will be our lamp. We will know in the fullness of our experience that the Lord is genuinely the Alpha and the Omega. He is the one who makes sense of the beginning and is the end.

It is this epic story that not only transforms our beliefs but our entire identity in the world. It is a different 'way of looking at the world'. And it is the church that needs to tell anew the story not only among its people but also in the world outside its walls. The story is not private – its claims touch all of life. It speaks to the world of work, to the world of leisure, to the world of the family. It is concerned with human flourishing and the place of justice in our common life together. It is a story that encourages a love for those who hate, to forgive those who seek to harm, and to work for reconciliation among alienated parties.

Recovering the plausibility of the biblical 'way of looking at the world' begins with small concrete steps. It cannot be an abstract or ethereal strategy. It is not simply believing a story, but being embedded in the story that makes the difference. That inevitably happens slowly across time. It requires a change of habits as well as a change of convictions. It comes from belonging not only to the present but gaining a sense of belonging to something that reaches into the past as well as far off into the future.

Plastic narratives are notoriously stories within generations and not across generations. Generational narratives tend to divide rather than unite. Christians buy into this distortion of their own narrative whenever they root their sense of identity generationally. Instead of conceiving an identity rooted in peer group units there should be a return to thinking of cross-generational units, consisting of people of different ages across diverse cultural geographies.

Concretely this means ecclesial communities encouraging generations to bump into each other and to encourage them to know their cultural genealogies. Local churches should think of ministry across cultural generations as well as across generations. The church needs to develop ways to let older folks be a part of the lives of younger folks, and younger folks to be involved in the lives of even younger folks, to find older mentors in the marketplace for younger individuals in the marketplace, and create opportunities for leadership in those younger generations. The church ought to be wary if age group peers are the primary mentors in discipleship or evangelism – or in the world of work, the world of the family, the world of education. This is not simply a pragmatic concern; it is to think about the practice of Christians in community theologically.

In the vinyl narratives of our age meals are often of the fast-food variety – both in terms of nutrition and speed. The investment of our lives in others across the table has been replaced by thinking of meals as simply a functional means to satisfying one's personal hunger. The recent renaissance of 'farm to table' traditions in the West comes as a mild rebuke to the gospel-believing church that too easily has been co-opted by the fast-food culture of late modernity. In that light might the church encourage people to eat meals together not simply as a means to meet new people, but as a celebration of the covenantal aspects of shared meals. Lives are so busy in our day that families eating together proves to be a major undertaking. Churches are no different. Blocking out time to share a meal among communities and in communities has profound spiritual consequences. It will not slow the world down but just may be one way to remind Christians of the covenant that does in fact bind them together. This would also have a profound impact upon the practice of the Lord's Supper.

In many of our plastic narratives the heart is deceived into thinking that it gets what it wants. The context of that deception is often that the individual is supreme and thereby is the rightful source of all final choices.[30] The church needs to be reminded that in a kingdom the king has final authority. The church is not a divine democracy. Not everyone gets a vote. And as the old adage suggests, a benevolent ruler is in fact the simplest and most efficient form of government. Individuals do not govern the church – God does. We all need to be reminded that the major decisions facing the church have already been made. And therefore the day-to-day logistical decisions must not be so emphasized that we lose sight of the eternal principles that have already been laid down for us by our Lord. I think this means helping people understand that their central stake in the church is not their right to express their opinions or to vote in a congregational meeting.

These suggestions should not be the specialty of church consultants or theologians, but of ordinary pastors and ordinary churches. Abstracted from the life of the church the biblical narrative loses its heart and soul. The confessions of the church inevitably become merely a statement of doctrines that protect the church from the outside world – defining simply who is 'in' and who is 'out', rather than giving identity to the church by giving to the church an entire 'way of looking at the world and living in the world'.

The gospel too often functions as one of the many competing and artificial narratives of our age – even and especially for churchgoing folk. Theologians have become technicians and engineers of the gospel, no longer finding their identity in and with the church. Pastors too quickly burn out in the midst of church conflicts and cultural insignificance. It is true that the church abandons the biblical narrative only at great peril to itself. It is also true that Christians abandon this narrative when it is only an abstract and artificial confession.

How is the biblical narrative to regain a place of prominence in a church that often thinks of it as irrelevant? Christians must first become convinced that it is good to regain a sense of the centrality of Scripture. This cannot be accomplished without much more deliberate biblical-theological strategy to reinvigorate our identity as images of the living God, in whom our greatest satisfaction can be found. We must also cease thinking of this as abstracted from the everyday living concrete realities of life. The gospel is to be lived out on the pages of ordinary life, reflecting the God who has acted out redemption on the pages of history. It cannot be sequestered behind the walls of the

---

[30] The radio phone-in, where everyone gets to voice their opinion regardless of its validity, is the characteristic genre of this narrative in our time.

church, though the church must function as the means to recover the living vitality of the biblical narrative.

If all of us are called to think theologically about the concrete habits of the church in which the gospel is narrated for our life in the world, it should also be said that we need to challenge the intellectual structures that give plausibility to the plastic narratives of our time. In our day this means, in part, confessing a mega-narrative in a time when all narratives of transcendence are suspect. But the attempt to deny all narratives of transcendence is of course itself a metanarrative, and if any lesson has been learned in the twentieth century it is that arguments of relativism are almost always self-referentially incoherent.[31] We must also be willing to say that the plastic narratives of the present moment are fatally flawed, even if they are the most common today. Our cultural conscience is one of many historically available forms of consciousness and cannot be privileged simply on the grounds that it is ours.[32]

If we are honest we must admit that there is an inherent dislike of the self-disclosure of God in every human being, and it is this reason that leads too often to a thousand different interpretations. We must expect that there will be different cultural instantiations of unbelief and idolatry. We should not expect our idols to look the same as everyone else's. If the lesson of the nineteenth-century secular prophets was that we are capable of creating God in our own image, the twentieth century has given us good evidence that we do this all the time. The human heart will always be restless until it finds the living God of the universe.

What the preceding argument has sought to accomplish is a slight cultural reconceptualization of sin for our time from that of breaking a law (since the notion of law is such a culturally contested notion) to the notion of idolatry – chasing after things that will not satisfy our deepest longings. We are controlled in our world by an implicit affirmation that our desires are worth satisfying. Christians need to make the apologetic case that not all our desires are worth satisfying and many of them are conflicting ones. The greatest and deepest desires, for significance, for security, for eternity, can be satisfied only by being found in God's redemptive grace in Christ.

---

[31] See A. Plantinga (1986: 16–93) for an extended explanation of self-referential incoherence.
[32] I take this to be Berger's (1969) central argument. Reading classical literature all too often reminds us of this truth. I may add this is one reason why reading is such an endangered activity in our time. Cf. Birkerts 1994.

To the contemporary flattening of all truth claims we must affirm that it is God who is universal and not the human interpretation project. All perspectives are not equal if there is a God who creates every living thing. His perspective ultimately is what counts. Put positively the biblical narrative, the story of God's redemption from Genesis to consummation, ought to be the heart of the church's identity and all those who find a place in that community. Without it we will be for ever defined by the plastic narratives of our times. Ironically it is the challenge of contested narratives in our time that may well reawaken us to the power of the mega-narrative of being images of the living God. And for that we thank the Lord for his strange providence.

Bibliography

Achtemeier, P. (1999), 'Gods Made with Hands: The New Testament and the Problem of Idolatry', *ExAud* 15, 43–61.

Ameriks, K. (2012), *Kant's Elliptical Path*, Oxford: Oxford University Press.

Anderson, B. W. (1977), 'A Stylistic Study of the Priestly Creation Story', in G. W. Coates and B. O. Long (eds.), *Canon and Authority: Essays in Old Testament Religion and Theology*, Philadelphia: Fortress, 148–162.

Assman, J. (1997), *Moses the Egyptian: The Memory of Egypt in Western Monotheism*, Cambridge, Mass.: Harvard University Press.

Bacchiocchi, S. (1998), *The Sabbath Under Crossfire: A Biblical Analysis of Recent Sabbath/Sunday Developments*, Berrien Springs: Biblical Perspectives.

Bailey, L. R. (1971), 'The Golden Calf', *HUCA* 42, 97–115.

Bailey, R. (1990), 'Acts 17:16–34', *RevExp* 87, 481–485.

Balthasar, H. U. von (1988), *Theo-Drama: Theological Dramatic Theory*, tr. G. Harrison, San Francisco: Ignatius.

Barr, J. (1968), 'The Image of God in the Book of Genesis – A Study in Terminology', *BJRL* 51, 11–26.

Barrett, C. K. (1974), 'Paul's Speech on the Areopagus', in M. Glasswell and E. F. Luke (eds.), *New Testament Christianity for Africa and the World*, London: SPCK, 69–77.

Barrett, W. (1986), *Death of the Soul: From Descartes to the Computer*, New York: Anchor.

Barth, K. (1957), 'Introductory Essay', in Feuerbach 1957: x–xi.

——— (1958), *Church Dogmatics* III/1, Edinburgh, T. & T. Clark.

——— (1975), *Church Dogmatics* I/1, *The Doctrine of the Word of God*, 2nd ed., ed. G. W. Bromiley and T. F. Torrance, Edinburgh: T. & T. Clark.

Bartholomew, C. G., and M. W. Goheen (2004a), *The Drama of Scripture: Finding Our Place in the Biblical Story*, Grand Rapids: Baker.

—— (2004b), 'Story and Biblical Theology', in C. Bartholomew, M. Healy, K. Möller and R. Parry (eds.), *Out of Egypt: Biblical Theology and Biblical Interpretation*, Milton Keynes: Paternoster, 144–171.

Barton, S. (2007), 'Food Rules, Sex Rules and the Prohibition of Idolatry. What's the Connection?', in S. Barton (ed.), *Idolatry: False Worship in the Bible, Early Judaism, and Christianity*, New York: T. & T. Clark, 141–162.

Batnitzky, L. (2000), *Idolatry and Representation: The Philosophy of Franz Rosenzweig Reconsidered*, Princeton: Princeton University Press.

Beale, G. K. (2004), *The Temple and the Church's Mission: A Biblical Theology of the Dwelling Place of God*, Leicester: Apollos; Downers Grove: InterVarsity Press.

—— (2008), *We Become What We Worship: A Biblical Theology of Idolatry*, Downers Grove: InterVarsity Press; Leicester: Apollos.

Beckerleg, C. (2009), 'The Image of God in Eden: The Creation of Mankind in Genesis 2:5–3:24 in Light of the mis pi pit pi and wpt-r Rituals of Mesopotamia and Ancient Egypt', PhD diss., Cambridge, Mass.: Harvard University.

Berger, P. (1967), *The Sacred Canopy: Elements of a Sociological Theory of Religion*, New York: Doubleday.

—— (1969), *A Rumor of Angels: Modern Society and the Rediscovery of the Supernatural*, New York: Doubleday.

—— (1979), *The Heretical Imperative: Contemporary Possibilities of Religious Affirmation*, New York: Doubleday.

Berkhof, L. (1939), *Systematic Theology*, Grand Rapids: Eerdmans.

Berkouwer, G. C. (1962), *Man: The Image of God*, Grand Rapids: Eerdmans.

Biguzzi, G. (1998), 'Ephesus, Its Artemision, Its Temple to the Flavian Emperors, and Idolatry in Revelation', *NovT* 40.3, 276–290.

Birkerts, S. (1994), *The Gutenberg Elegies: The Fate of Reading in an Electronic Age*, Boston: Faber and Faber.

Blocher, H. (1984), *In the Beginning*, Leicester: Inter-Varsity Press; Downers Grove: InterVarsity Press.

Bolsinger, T. (2004), *It Takes a Church to Raise a Christian: How the Community of God Transforms Lives*, Grand Rapids: Brazos.

Bonnington, M. (2007), 'Fleeing *Idolatry*: Social Embodiment of Anti-*Idolatry* in the First Century', in S. Barton (ed.), *Idolatry: False Worship in the Bible, Early Judaism, and Christianity*, New York: T. & T. Clark, 107–119.

Borgmann, A. (2003), *Power Failure: Christianity in the Culture of Technology*, Grand Rapids: Brazos.

Bray, G. (1991), 'The Significance of God's Image in Man', *TynB* 42.2, 195–225.

Brooks, D. (2008), 'Harmony and the Dream', *New York Times*, 11 Aug.

—————— (2012), *The Social Animal*, New York: Random House.

Brown, W. P. (1993), *Structure, Role, and Ideology in the Hebrew and Greek Texts of Genesis 1:1–2:3*, SBLDS 132, Atlanta: Scholars Press.

Bruce, F. F. (1988), *Acts of the Apostles*, Grand Rapids: Eerdmans.

Brueggemann, W. (1982), *Genesis: A Bible Commentary for Teaching and Preaching*, IBC, Atlanta: John Knox.

—————— (1988), *Israel's Praise: Doxology Against Idolatry and Ideology*, Philadelphia: Fortress.

—————— (1997), *Theology of the Old Testament*, Minneapolis: Fortress.

Buber, M. (1970), *I and Thou*, New York: Scribner (originally published as *Ich und Du* in 1920).

Calvin, J. (1960), *The Institutes of the Christian Religion*, ed. J. T. McNeill, Philadelphia: Westminster.

Cassuto, U. (1961–4), *A Commentary on the Book of Genesis*, vol. 1, Jerusalem: Magnes.

—————— (1967), *A Commentary on the Book of Exodus*, Jerusalem: Magnes.

Childs, B. (1974), *Exodus: A Commentary*, London: SCM.

Clapp, R. (ed.) (1997), *The Consuming Passion*, Downers Grove: InterVarsity Press.

Clifford, R. (1994), *Creation Accounts in the Ancient Near East and in the Bible*, CBQMS 26, Washington, D.C.: Catholic Biblical Association of America.

Clines, D. J. A. (1998), 'Humanity as the Image of God', in *On the Way to the Postmodern: Old Testament Essays, 1967–1998*, vol. 2, Sheffield: Sheffield Academic Press, 447–497.

Cloy, N. C. (1997), 'Hellenistic Philosophies and the Preaching of the Resurrection (Acts 17:18, 32)', *NovT* 39, 21–39.

Collins, F. (2006), *The Language of God: A Scientist Presents Evidence for Belief*, New York: Free.

Copleston, F. (1993a), *A History of Philosophy*, vol. 4, New York: Doubleday.

—————— (1993b), *A History of Philosophy*, vol. 5, New York: Doubleday.

────── (1993c), *A History of Philosophy*, vol. 6, New York: Doubleday.

Cross, F. M. (1998), 'Kinship and Covenant in Ancient Israel', in F. M. Cross (ed.), *From Epic to Canon: History and Literature in Ancient Israel*, Baltimore: Johns Hopkins University Press, 3–21.

Dahl, N. (1966), 'The Story of Abraham in Luke-Acts', in L. Keck and L. Martin (eds.), *Studies in Luke-Acts*, Nashville: Abingdon, 139–158.

Davies, O., and D. Turner (eds.) (2002), *Silence and the Word: Negative Theology and Incarnation*, New York: Cambridge University Press.

Davis, M. (2003), 'Acts 17:16–34', *Int* 57.2, 64–68.

Donaldson, T. L. (1981), 'Moses Typology and the Sectarian Nature of Anti-Judaism in Acts 7', *JSNT* 12, 27–52.

Dumbrell, W. (1989), 'Creation, Covenant and Work', *ERT* 13, 137–156.

Dunham, R. (2006), 'Acts 17:16–34', *Int* 202–206.

Eire, C. M. N. (1986), *War Against Idols: The Reformation of Worship from Erasmus to Calvin*, Cambridge: Cambridge University Press.

Ellul, J. (1985), *The Humiliation of the Word*, Grand Rapids: Eerdmans.

Elshtain, J. B. (1993), 'The New Tape File II', *First Things* 32, April, 12–13.

Evans, C., and J. Sanders (1993), *Luke and Scripture: The Function of Sacred Tradition in Luke-Acts*, Minneapolis: Fortress.

Fatoorchi, P. (2008), 'Avicenna on the Human Self-Consciousness', *International Ibn Sina Symposium Papers*, Istanbul: Ekim, 28–41.

Feuerbach, L. (1957), *The Essence of Christianity*, New York: Harper & Row (originally Leipzig: Otto Wigand, 1841).

────── (1981), *Thoughts on Death and Immortality*, Oakland: University of California Press.

Fisher, L. (1963), 'The Temple Quarter', *JSS* 8, 34–41.

Fjellman, S. (1992), *Vinyl Leaves: Walt Disney World and America*, Boulder: Westview.

Frei, H. (1974), *The Eclipse of Biblical Narrative*, New Haven: Yale University Press.

Friedman, M. (1999), *Reconsidering Logical Positivism*, Cambridge: Cambridge University Press.

Gaffin, R. (1987), *Resurrection and Redemption*, Phillipsburg: P. & R.

Garrett, D. (1992), *Rethinking Genesis*, Grand Rapids: Baker.

Gay, C. (1998), *The Way of the (Modern) World*, Grand Rapids: Eerdmans.

Geller, J. (1997), 'Idols, Fetishes and Foreskins: The Other in Religion', *Religion* 27, 117–122.

Gergen, K. (1990), *The Saturated Self: Dilemmas of Identity in Contemporary Life*, New York: Basic.

Goffman, E. (1959), *The Presentation of Self in Everyday Life*, Garden City, N.Y.: Doubleday.

Grenz, S. (2001), *The Social God and the Relational Self*, Louisville: Westminster John Knox.

—— (2004), 'Jesus as the Imago Dei: Image-of-God Christology and the Non-Linear Linearity of Theology', *JETS* 47.4, 617–628.

Griffin, D. R. (1989a), 'Introduction: Varieties of Postmodern Theology', in D. R. Griffin, W. A. Beadslee and J. Holland (eds.), *Varieties of Postmodern Theology*, Albany: State University of New York Press, 1–8.

—— (1989b), 'Postmodern Theology and A/Theology: A Response to Mark C. Taylor', in D. R. Griffin, W. A. Beadslee and J. Holland (eds.), *Varieties of Postmodern Theology*, Albany: State University of New York Press, 29–62.

Gunkel, H. (1910), *Genesis*, HKAT 1.1, Göttingen: Vandenhoeck & Ruprecht.

Halbertal, M. (1992), *Idolatry*, Cambridge, Mass.: Harvard University Press.

—— (1998), 'Coexisting with the Enemy: Jews and Pagans in the Mishnah', in G. N. Stanton and G. G. Stroumsa (eds.), *Tolerance and Intolerance in Early Judaism and Christianity*, Cambridge: Cambridge University Press, 159–171.

Hamilton, V. P. (1990), *The Book of Genesis: Chapters 1–17*, NICNT, Grand Rapids: Eerdmans.

Hare, J. (2009), *God and Morality: A Philosophical History*, Oxford: Wiley-Blackwell.

Harrison, N. V. (2002), 'Human Community as an Image of the Holy Trinity', *StVTQ* 46.4, 347–364.

Hart, I. (1995), 'Genesis 1:1–2:3 as a Prologue to the Book of Genesis', *TynB* 46.2, 315–336.

Hart, T. (2000), 'Imagination and Responsible Reading', in C. Bartholomew, C. Green and K. Möller (eds.), *Renewing Biblical Interpretation*, Carlisle: Paternoster, 307–334.

Harvey, V. A. (1995), *Feuerbach and the Interpretation of Religion*, New York: Cambridge University Press.

Hasel, G. R. (1974), 'The Polemical Nature of the Genesis Cosmology', *EvQ* 46, 81–102.

Hegel, M. (1977), *The Phenomenology of Spirit*, Oxford: Clarendon.

Helm, P. (1995), 'Review of Halbertal and Margalit, Idolatry', *Mind* 414, 419–422.

Hendrix, R. (1990), 'A Literary Structural Analysis of the Golden Calf Episode in Exodus 32:1–33:6', *AUSS* 28.3, 211–217.

Hengel, M. (1989), *The Zealots: Investigations Into the Jewish Freedom Movement in the Period from Herod I Until 70 A.D.*, Edinburgh: T. & T. Clark.

Hodge, C. (1986), *Systematic Theology*, Grand Rapids: Eerdmans (originally New York: Scribners, 1873).

Hooker, M. (1960), 'Adam in Romans 1', *NTS* 6.4, 297–306.

Horton, M. (2002), *Covenant and Eschatology: The Divine Drama*, Louisville: Westminster John Knox.

—— (2005), *Lord and Servant: A Covenant Christology*, Louisville: Westminster John Knox.

—— (2006), *God of Promise: Introducing Covenant Theology*, Grand Rapids: Baker.

Hugenberger, G. (1994), *Marriage as a Covenant: A Study of Biblical Law and Ethics Governing Marriage, Developed from the Perspective of Malachi*, Leiden: Brill.

Hughes, P. E. (1989), *The True Image: The Origin and Destiny of Man in Christ*, Grand Rapids: Eerdmans.

Hurwitz, V. (1992), *I Have Built You an Exalted House: Temple Building in the Bible in the Light of Mesopotamian and North-West Semitic Writings*, Sheffield: JSOT Press.

Johnson, E. (1990), *Expository Hermeneutics*, Grand Rapids: Zondervan.

Jónsson, G. A. (1988), *The Image of God: Genesis 1:26–28 in a Century of Old Testament Research*, Stockholm: Almqvist & Wiksell.

Keller, T. (2009), *Counterfeit Gods: The Empty Promises of Money, Sex and Power and the Only Hope That Matters*, New York: Dutton.

Kelsey, D. (2006), 'Personal Bodies: A Theological Anthropological Proposal', in R. Lints, M. Horton and M. R. Talbot (eds.), *Personal Identity in Theological Perspective*, Grand Rapids: Eerdmans, 139–158.

Keyes, D. (1992), 'The Idol Factory', in Os Guinness and John Seel (eds.), *No God But God*, Chicago: Moody, 3–12.

Klauck, H. J. (2000), *The Religious Context of Early Christianity*, Edinburgh: T. & T. Clark.

Kline, M. (1963), *Treaty of the Great King*, Grand Rapids: Eerdmans.

—— (1980), *Images of the Spirit*, Grand Rapids: Eerdmans.

—— (2006), *Kingdom Prologue: Genesis Foundations for a Covenantal Worldview*, Eugene: Wipf & Stock.

Kutsko, J. F. (1998), 'Will the Real *selem elohim* Please Stand Up? The Image of God in the Book of Ezekiel', *SBLSP* 37, pt 1, 86–105.

Lasch, C. (1986), *The Minimal Self*, New York: Norton.

Levenson, J. (1984), 'The Temple and the World', *JR* 64, 139–158.

—— (1988), *Creation and the Persistence of Evil: The Jewish Drama of Divine Omnipotence*, San Francisco: Harper & Row.

Lewis, T. (2011), 'Religion and Demythologization in Hegel's Phenomenology of Spirit', in D. Moyar and M. Quante (eds.), *Hegel's Phenomenology of Spirit: A Critical Guide*, Cambridge: Cambridge University Press, 192–209.

Lindbeck, G. (1984), *The Nature of Doctrine*, Philadelphia: Westminster.

Lints, R. (1993), *The Fabric of Theology*, Grand Rapids: Eerdmans.

—— (2000), 'The Vinyl Narratives: The Metanarratives of Postmodernity and the Recovery of a Churchly Theology', in M. Horton, *A Confessing Theology for Postmodern Times*, Wheaton: Crossway, 91–110.

—— (2011), 'The Strange Wisdom of Diversity: Learning to Live Together in the Ecclesial Square', in M. Volf, C. Constantineanu, M. Măcelaru and K. Š. Osijek (eds.), *First the Kingdom of God*, Osijek, Croatia: Evandeoski Teoloski Fakultet, 399–420.

—— (2013), 'A Post-Partisan Partisan Ecclesiology', in R. Lints, *The Renewing of the Evangelical Mission*, Grand Rapids: Eerdmans, 161–188.

Louth, A (ed.) (2001), *Genesis 1–11*, ACCS, Downers Grove: InterVarsity Press.

McBride, S. D. (2000), 'Divine Protocol: Genesis 1:1–2:3 as Prologue to the Pentatuech', in W. P. Brown and S. D. McBride (eds.), *God Who Creates*, Grand Rapids: Eerdmans, 3–41.

McFague, S. (1982), *Metaphorical Theology: Models of God in Religious Language*, Philadelphia: Fortress.

McGrath, A. (2009), *A Fine-Tuned Universe: The Quest for God in Science and Theology: The 2009 Gifford Lectures*, Louisville: Westminster John Knox.

McGuckin, J. (2004), *The Westminster Handbook to Patristic Theology*, Louisville: Westminster/John Knox.

Marcus, J. (2006), 'Idolatry in the New Testament', *Int* 60.2, 152–164.

Mare, H. (1971), 'Acts 7: Jewish or Samaritan in Character', *WTJ* 34.1, 1–21.

Marshall, B. D. (1990), 'Absorbing the World: Christianity and the Universe of Truths', in B. D. Marshall (ed.), *Theology and Dialogue: Essays in Conversation with George Lindbeck*, Notre Dame: University of Notre Dame Press, 69–102.

Mathews, K. (1996), *Genesis 1–11:26*, NAC, Nashville: Broadman & Holman.

Maxwell, J. M. (1972), 'In the "Image" and "Likeness" of God', *JBL* 91, 290–304.

May, H. F. (1976), *The Enlightenment in America*, New York: Oxford University Press.

Mendenhall, G. E. (1955), *Law and Covenant in Israel and the Ancient Near East*, Pittsburgh: Biblical Colloquium.

Miles, J. (1995), *God: A Biography*, New York: Alfred Knopf.

Moxnes, H. (1995), 'He Saw That the City was Full of Idols, Acts 17:16: Visualizing the World of the First Christians', in D. Hellhom, H. Moxnes and T. K. Seim (eds.), *Mighty Minorities: Minorities in Early Christianity*, Oslo: Scandinavian University Press, 107–132.

Moyer, D., and M. Quante (eds.) (2011), *Hegel's Phenomenology of Spirit: A Critical Guide*, Cambridge: Cambridge University Press.

Nash, L. (1994), *Believers in Business*, Nashville: Thomas Nelson.

Niccol, A. (2002), *Simone*, directed Andrew Niccol, performed Al Pacino, New Line Cinema.

Niehaus, J. (1995), *God at Sinai*, Grand Rapids: Zondervan.

Nietzsche, F. (1974), *The Gay Science*, New York: Random House (originally Leipzig: 1881).

———— (1987), *On the Genealogy of Morals*, New York: Vintage (originally Leipzig: 1887).

Ortlund Jr., R. C. (1996), *God's Unfaithful Wife: A Biblical Theology of Spiritual Adultery*, Leicester: Apollos; Downers Grove: InterVarsity Press.

Peirce, C. S. (1991), 'On the Nature of Signs', in J. Hoopes (ed.), *Peirce On Signs: Writings on Semiotics by Charles Sanders Peirce*, Chapel Hill: University of North Carolina Press, 141–144.

Pelikan, J. (2005), *Acts: A Theological Commentary*, Grand Rapids: Brazos.

Phillips, T. E. (2003), 'Creation Sin and Curse and the People of God: An Intertextual Reading of Genesis 1–12 and Acts 1–7', *HBT* 25, 146–160.

Plantinga, A. (1986), 'Reason and Belief in God', in A. Plantinga and N. Wolterstorff (eds.), *Faith and Rationality*, Notre Dame: University of Notre Dame Press, 16–93.

Plantinga, C. (1995), *Not the Way It's Supposed to Be*, Grand Rapids: Eerdmans.

Price, S. R. F. (1984), *Rituals and Power: The Roman Imperial Cult in Asia Minor*, Cambridge: Cambridge University Press.

Putnam, R. (2000), *Bowling Alone: The Collapse and Revival of American Communities*, New York: Simon & Schuster.

—— (2001), *Bowling Alone: The Collapse and Revival of American Communities*, New York: Simon & Schuster.

Rad, G. von (1972), *Genesis*, OTL, London: Westminster John Knox.

Ridderbos, H. (1957), 'The Meaning of Genesis 1', *FUQ* 4, 221–234.

Rorty, R. (ed.) (1967), *The Linguistic Turn*, Chicago: University of Chicago Press.

—— (1981), *Philosophy and the Mirror of Nature*, Princeton: Princeton University Press.

Rosner, B. (1991), 'The Concept of Idolatry', *Them* 24, 21–30.

—— (2009), *Greed as Idolatry*, Grand Rapids: Eerdmans.

Rowe, C. K. (2005), 'New Testament Iconography? Situating Paul in the Absence of Material Evidence', in A. Weissenreider, F. Wendt and P. von Gemunden (eds.), *Picturing the New Testament: Studies in Ancient Visual Images*, Tübingen: Mohr Siebeck, 289–312.

Rumscheidt, M. (1999), 'The God of Freedom and the Slavery of Idolatry', *ExAud* 15, 91–102.

Samuelson, N. (1992), *The First Seven Days: A Philosophical Commentary on the Creation in Genesis*, Atlanta: Scholars Press.

Sawyer, J. F. A. (1974), 'The Meaning of "In the Image of God" in Genesis 1–11', *JTS* 25, 418–426.

Seeskin, K. (1995), *No Other Gods: The Modern Struggle Against Idolatry*, West Orange: Berhman House.

Sproul, R. C. (1974), *The Psychology of Atheism*, Minneapolis: Bethany.

Stadler, F. (2001), *The Vienna Circle: Studies in the Origins, Development, and Influence of Logical Empiricism*, Vienna: Springer.

Stevens, M. (1998), *The Rise of the Image, the Fall of the World*, New York: Oxford University Press.

Stordalen, T. (2000), *Echoes of Eden*, Leuven: Peeters.

Stout, J. (1981), *The Flight from Authority: Religion Morality and the Quest for Autonomy*, Notre Dame: Notre Dame Press.

Strong, A. H. (1886), *Systematic Theology*, Rochester: E. R. Andrews.

Sweeney, J. (2002), 'Stephen's Speech (Acts 7:2–53): Is It as "Anti-Temple" as Is Frequently Alleged?', *TrinJ* 23, NS, 185–210.

Tseelon, E. (1992), 'Is the Presented Self Sincere? Goffman, Impression Management and the Postmodern Self', *Theory, Culture and Society* 9.2, 115–128.

Vanhoozer, K. (2005), *The Drama of Doctrine: A Canonical Linguistic Approach to Christian Doctrine*, Louisville: Westminster John Knox.

Volf, M. (1996), *Exclusion and Embrace*, Nashville: Abingdon.

Vos, G. (1948), *Biblical Theology*, Grand Rapids: Eerdmans.

Ward, T. (2002), *Word and Supplement: Speech Acts, Biblical Texts and the Sufficiency of Scripture*, New York: Oxford University Press.

Warden, D. (1991), 'Imperial Persecution and the Dating of 1 Peter and Revelation', *JETS* 34, 203–212.

Weinfeld, M. (1981), 'Sabbath, Temple and the Enthronement of the Lord – The Problem of the Sitz im Leben of Genesis 1:1–2:3', in A. Caquot and M. Delcor (eds.), *Mélanges bibliques et orientaux en l'honneur de M. Henrie Cazelles*, Kevelaer: Butzon & Bercker, 501–512.

Wenham, G. (1987), *Genesis 1–15*, WBC, Waco: Word.

Westermann, C. (1984), *Genesis 1–11: A Commentary*, Minneapolis: Augsburg Fortress.

——— (1992), *Genesis: An Introduction*, Minneapolis: Augsburg Fortress.

Westphal, M. (1994), *Suspicion and Faith: The Religious Uses of Modern Atheism*, Grand Rapids: Eerdmans.

Wilken, R. (2005), *The Spirit of Early Christian Thought: Seeking the Face of God*, New Haven: Yale University Press.

Williams, J. P. (2000), *Denying Divinity: Apophasis in the Patristic Tradition and Soto Zen Buddhist Traditions*, New York: Oxford University Press.

Willimon, W. (2010), *Acts: A Bible Commentary for Teaching and Preaching*, IBC, Louisville: Westminster John Knox.

Wilson, S. G. (1973), *Gentiles and the Gentile Mission in Luke-Acts*, New York: Cambridge University Press.

Witherington, B. (1998), *The Acts of the Apostles: A Socio-Rhetorical Commentary*, Grand Rapids: Eerdmans.

Wolde, E. van (1996), *Stories of the Beginning: Genesis 1–11 and Other Creation Stories*, tr. J. Bowden, London: SCM.

Wolterstorff, N. (1984), *Reason Within the Bounds of Religion*, Grand Rapids: Eerdmans.

——— (1995), *Divine Discourse: Philosophical Reflections on the Claim That God Speaks*, Cambridge: Cambridge University Press.

—— (2004), 'The Unity Behind the Canon', in C. Helmer and C. Landmesser (eds.), *One Scripture or Many? Canon from Biblical, Theological and Philosophical Perspectives*, Oxford: Oxford University Press, 217–232.

Wright, N. T. (1992), *The Climax of the Covenant: Christ and the Law in Pauline Theology*, Minneapolis: Fortress.

—— (2008), *Acts for Everyone*, vol. 1, Louisville: Westminster John Knox.

Zanker, P. (1998), *The Power of Images in the Age of Augustus*, Ann Arbor: University of Michigan Press.

Index of authors

Index of Scripture references

187